FREEDOM

MW01287238

"If New Thought is to claim a space among liberation theology of the 21st century," David Alexander writes, "it will require examining deeply who we are, who we want to be, and getting honest about who we have been in the recent past."

Is New Thought a liberation theology? Despite the fact that our world is in desperate need of massive change, many practitioners treat New Thought as a convenient excuse to take no action, believing "those people" brought their conditions on themselves, so they have to liberate themselves by themselves.

Alexander traces the roots of New Thought back to its originators, making the case that New Thought is indeed transformative and designed to address the inequities of our times. He explodes some of the more powerful myths that cloud the view of New Thought as liberation theology, leading to an inescapable conclusion: *We must take action.* This leads to one major problem with Alexander's book: While reading it, you may find your comfort zone eroding.

Part historical reference, part philosophical treatise, and part liberation manifesto, *Freedom from Discord* charts a clear path to the spiritual and societal transformations needed for a 21st century that works for all living beings.

– Shariff Abdullah, JD
Founder, Commonway Institute
Author of *Creating a World That Works for All* and
Birthing the Nation of Gaia

Rev. David Alexander is an intrepid myth buster. In his book, *Freedom from Discord: The Promise of New Thought Liberation Theology,* he shares a truth only a believer could tell, revealing the fundamental historical foundations supporting the authentic roots of New Thought. He deftly deconstructs false cultural norms and the spiritual pride binding us to them, and in the process reveals the obfuscation, gaslighting, and mass resistance to the basic tenets of liberation theology.

Rev. David boldly unfurls the fabric of our roots, establishing that Ancient Wisdom was nurtured in Black and Brown cultures. He busts five modern myths, revealing how far we strayed from our Ancient Wisdom roots in liberation theology. He asserts that these are the myths we "must let go of to manifest a world that works for all." His compelling thesis leaves us, in the words of Martha and the Vandellas, "nowhere to run, nowhere to hide."

– Rev. Dr. Andriette Earl
Founding Spiritual Leader, Heart and Soul Center of Light

With keen insight, Rev. Dr. David Alexander gives us a comprehensive analysis on how to participate in spiritually grounded social justice activism from a place of faith, not fear. *Freedom from Discord: The Promise of New Thought Liberation Theology* serves as a tapestry of the past, an anchor for the present, and a beacon for the future. It calls us up from complacency and calls us out of complicity to actively engage in ushering in the beloved community. The wisdom of Dr. Alexander's experience, infused throughout the book, gives it a moral authority upon which to stand. It is well worth the read.

– Rev. Deborah L. Johnson,
author of *The Sacred YES* and *Your Deepest Intent*

In *Freedom from Discord,* Rev. David Alexander brings a radically inquisitive and thoughtful perspective and framework to the idea of New Thought liberation theology and the possibilities and potential within it to step up to, meet, and respond to the call of our times. This inspires me, as the bedrock of the Civil Rights Movement was *agape,* or unconditional love, and part of my mission when I founded Agape International Spiritual Center in 1986 was to help give birth to the beloved community as imagined by the Rev. Dr. Martin Luther King Jr., a world that works for the highest and best *in* and *for* all of us. This textbook has the promise of ushering in fresh thoughts and ideas that expand upon that from a New Thought/Ancient Wisdom perspective.

As we know, the limitations of the human mind condition us to focus on what we currently see in the manifest realm as reality. This includes all of the challenges and "isms" that result from contracted race consciousness and the seeming complexity, opacity, and intractability of the human social structures, systems, and hierarchies that maintain them. The fear these behemoths can engender among individuals can be blinding, preventing us from seeing above and beyond the challenges, rendering us feeling utterly disempowered to do anything about them.

But when we are blind to or refuse to see, much less confront, a challenge, fear, or limitation, we cannot even begin to fathom a radically new view of life, much less receive inspiration from our Source Energy. We know this through the inner work we continually do as spiritual practitioners in New Thought and metaphysics—which is why we practice. Yet, that is exactly why each of our souls incarnated here: to see with our Divine Eye behind the eye, above and beyond what has materialized, and consciously expand all of life through the grounding of the universal laws of inclusivity and unconditional love and oneness. As above, so below.

Let us open our hearts and minds to the expansive ideas laid out within these pages. Let us eagerly explore, study, and discuss the ideas brought forth with a beginner's mind and a joyful anticipation that something wonderful seeks to emerge through us and as us on our individual and collective journeys to expand humanity outward, upward, and forward.

Rev. David said it best when he wrote: "I believe that New Thought provides a powerful libertative witness to the power within each one of us to radically change the world through personal and collective awakening." This, I believe, is the next movement and moment for our New Thought/ Ageless Wisdom teachings and communities.

– Michael Bernard Beckwith
Founder and CEO, Agape International Spiritual Center

THE PROMISE OF NEW THOUGHT
LIBERATION THEOLOGY

FREEDOM
FROM
DISCORD

REV. DAVID ALEXANDER, DD

FOREWORD BY REV. KEVIN ROSS
AFTERWORD BY BISHOP YVETTE FLUNDER

SPIRITUAL
LIVING
PRESS

Spiritual Living Press, an imprint of Centers for Spiritual Living
Lakewood, Colorado 80226
www.Shop.CSL.org

Printed in the United States of America
Published March 2024

Editor: Julie Mierau, JM Wordsmith
Design/Layout: Holli Sharp, Centers for Spiritual Living

ISBN paperback: 978-1-956198-42-3

ISBN eBook: 978-1-956198-43-0

DEDICATION

For my children, Josh and William:
A better world for you is tied to the liberation of
humanity from the disease of disconnection.

---

*The ultimate goal in life is a complete
emancipation from discord of every nature
and this goal is sure to be attained by all.*

— *Ernest Holmes,* Can We Talk to God?

ACKNOWLEDGMENTS

First and foremost, I extend my gratitude to my wife, Patience, and to our children, who sacrifice more than they should have to in support of my calling as a minister. Patience believed in this project before I did and pushed me out of the house on numerous occasions to write.

I also am supported by an amazing Board of Trustees at Spiritual Living Center of Atlanta—my deep gratitude for your service and dedication and support. Thank you for calling me to Atlanta. I believe it is a calling of divine alignment for this sacred time, and I am humbled to work in the cradle of the Civil Rights Movement.

To all my teachers, guides, mentors, and supporters over the years, you know who you are, as do I. None of us stand alone. We stand with and because others made a way, shared their wisdom and their platform, and put wind into our sails.

I am a humble product of public schools, Boys and Girls Club, YMCA, spiritual community, and a single mother working night and day to raise two boys. Thank you, Mom, for being my biggest fan and always knowing the best for my journey.

Numerous individuals served in the each of these sectors as volunteers, mentors, and teachers. I have been shaped by them all. In particular, I want to call out the following: Jim and Carol Campbell (Albuquerque Youth Group leaders), Rev. Bob Henderson (Valley of the Sun Church of Religious Science), Rev. Patrick Pollard (sharing his pulpit for my first sermon), Rev. Dr. Clancy Blakemore (Holmes Institute Campus Dean), Rev. Dr. Harry Morgan Moses (co-laborer and guide through my launch in ministry).

Dr. Shariff Abdullah's work changed my consciousness completely. Dr. Michael Bernard Beckwith always sees me. Bishop Yvette Flunder and TFAM called me in as kin and held (and hold) me to account as co-laborer. There are countless others, and I trust you know who you are.

I love each of you so.

Finally, I acknowledge and offer my gratitude to the late Bishop Carlton D. Pearson, whose life and legacy live in my heart and mind forever.

IN GRATITUDE

My desire is that this book will stand as a valuable contribution toward expanded consciousness, radical inclusion, and justice from a New Thought perspective. I have long held the conviction that New Thought as a spiritual system and pathway of understanding the laws of consciousness has much to offer to the work of justice. Recently, someone asked in an online forum what was the best book on social justice from a New Thought perspective. I replied, *"The one I am writing."* Others listed classic works on liberation theology and social justice, but none from a New Thought consciousness perspective, save one, the other answer I gave, *Creating a World That Works for All* by Shariff Abdullah.

In 2005, Shariff was the keynote speaker for a United Church of Religious Science conference, with the theme "Creating a World that Works for Everyone." It was there that I met Dr. Shariff, who happened to be based in Portland, Oregon. I made sure I was first in line for his book signing. I devoured the book, and soon we met for coffee in Portland to further the kinship. That coffee meeting become a monthly, sometimes weekly, occasion for the next fifteen years. Over the years, we discussed everything from personal successes and failures to finding solutions to all the world problems, the shortcomings of New Thought, the approaches to working for justice, and politics.

Shariff's was the only body of work I was aware of that sought to put real-world teeth to the high-minded vision of a world that works for all and tie it all back to the inner work and responsibility of consciousness. To this day, his is still the most underrated and under-appreciated body of work within both justice communities and expanded-consciousness spiritual communities. Shariff's work was pioneering, and I owe a great debt of gratitude for his work, his friendship, and his contribution to the consciousness and direction of my ministry.

With Shariff's work as the ground floor, there remained a need to look at New Thought through a liberation lens, to view its emergence and responsiveness as emblematic of all liberation movements and thereby reclaim its prophetic zeal. Likewise we will look to frame a new story for the

21st century on the role of inclusive spirituality in a social justice movement for the 21st century and beyond.

With this book, I offer my contributions to the movement for social justice, with a focus on the role of spirituality in this work. I offer it as a love letter to the spiritual movement I love and have dedicated my life to, the same movement that must make some critical changes to survive and remain relevant in a rising world consciousness that is seeking new answers to dying paradigms.

TABLE OF CONTENTS

FOREWORD

Through the decades I have circled the sun and inhabited the Earth, traversing its spectacular topographies in both its northern and southern hemispheres, engaged with people of all strata—the rich and the poor, the powerful and those marginalized from power, the religious and nonreligious, the famous and the obscure—I continually find that people want to be identified with peace. This is both an honorable personal aspiration and a noble societal project.

On its face, it seems those who pursue peace consider themselves to be engaging in the most selfless enterprise, that which has the greatest benefit to humanity. And yet, based on the recorded history of the world, peace never saunters in on the tiptoes of ease and eventuality. Historically, more often than not, the path to peace is littered with shards of glass, landmines, starving babies with swollen bellies, polluted air and water, the lynching tree, sickness and disease, terrorism and hostage negotiations, and a bloody trail of the young, whose fragile uniformed bodies serve as the frontline for a nationalistic elite with a thirst for profit.

And while people like me insist on mostly identifying with that "Get-Along-Gang-Care-Bear-We-Are-the-World" kind of peace, we tend to look away from the realities involved in building it. We fast forward through the difficult parts of the process, demonizing such parts as "not spiritual" or labeling them "too political," and then we return for the ceremonial feel-good resolve.

For instance, we enjoy watching the Opening Ceremonies of the Olympics, where there are international displays of global harmony and universal kinship, but we look away from the fact that many Olympic host cities criminalize and imprison the unhoused to tidy up for international guests. And while we would prefer not to know that, it is our spiritual pole vaulting over the brutal facts into our closed-eyed, hand-holding circles that could unwittingly contribute to the dangerous bypassing of justice that so often is the silent saboteur of peace.

And it is to us—the well-meaning, high-minded, peace-loving pacifist-types—that I believe my dear brother, the Rev. Dr. David Alexander, speaks to with this book. There is no doubt whatsoever that we possess a sincere belief in and desire for peace, just like everybody else. And like so many others, we simply would not like to bother with the details. Our peace is an esoteric, visionary, apolitical, nonviolent, noncontroversial, consensus-building, silent, non-upsetting, sing-along type of peace. We sing, "Let there be peace on Earth and let it begin with me." However, what we really mean is, "Let there be peace on Earth and let it begin with me—but don't hold me to it."

We would rather isolate ourselves in the safe and speedy elevator to the top floor of peace, while the actual builders of peace take the stairs. And that long upward stairway to peace is called justice. As Dr. Cornel West said, "Justice is what love looks like in person."

And in our New Thought Ancient Wisdom circles, justice is often a word missing from our metaphysical lexicon. It is new for us to closely examine the structural, symbolic, and cultural injustices that serve as societal barriers to peace, because we have been mostly oriented to reducing all of society to the individuation of experience. Yet, our greater sense of self is in relation to one another and the ways in which we habitually fail at holding each other as fully human, fully equal, and fully free get encoded into society as systemic injustice, oppression, inequality, and inequity. These barriers to peace perhaps start on the individual level, but undoing the barriers will take a collective consciousness and a public effort.

The truth is, we love those stair-taking peace emissaries whose expanded consciousness and public effort make them iconic. The Reverend Dr. Martin Luther King Jr., President Nelson Mandela, His Holiness the Dalai Lama, Jesus, the Pope, Malala, and Rosa Parks are just a few examples. Each of these individuals found a way to fully integrate their religious and spiritual views, their core values, their philosophical, sociological, and political worldviews into their embodied personalities and through their actions. We love to celebrate them because they give us a glimpse of the coming attractions of our own matured potential, whether it frightens us or not. We like them because we are like them. We just don't know how to be like them.

This became abundantly clear to me in 2017, when I attended a conference in San Diego, California, at The Unity Center, a flagship Unity church led by the Reverend Wendy Craig Purcell. The Association for Global New Thought (AGNT) sponsored the conference, which drew hundreds of ordained ministers, credentialed practitioners, and elected laity.

One of our sessions focused on ways our leaders could be a beneficial presence on the planet and play a greater role in leading the change we wish to see. Several leaders praised the handful of us in our movement who engage in social justice work. However, they expressed fear, hesitation, and indifference when it came to seeing themselves becoming more involved in issues that seemed too politically charged, or too divisive, or that would reveal where they stood on a controversial issue. They feared a range of repercussions, including causing a rift in their congregations, losing key members and financial support, getting fired by their board of trustees, jeopardizing the church's tax exemption status, as well as no longer being seen as a spiritual leader but rather as a political one. Most, however, agreed that something more needs to be done to move the world beyond today's dangerous state of polarization and violence. They believed they would be willing to be engaged if they were better equipped to do so.

In short, it is not that our credentialed leaders want to completely avoid the stairs to building peace, rather I find that our leaders don't feel fully prepared to move outside their traditional pastoral and devotional roles to bring about social change. They tend to view people like me as exceptions.

Part of what makes me extra-normative as a Unity minister is my formal undergraduate studies at Morehouse College, where I earned a BA in Religious Studies and was formally trained in the prophetic nonviolent traditions of Martin Luther King Jr., Mohandus K. Gandhi, and Daisaku Ikeda. I have fifteen years of professional development experience, working with bonafide community organizers in California, intentionally building interfaith bridges by educating myself on social issues affecting people in countries where I don't live, with people whose religion I don't practice and whose culture is far different from mine. Most recently, I graduated with a Master's Degree in Religion and Public Life from Harvard Divinity School.

All of this preparation provides me with an extra-normative under-standing and a working knowledge of how to operationalize my deepest convictions about peace through my ministry, my political activity, my writings, and my activism. It is an embodied process that takes the stairs, but not alone. Like all such processes, it can be learned when there is a committed and passionate desire to grow spiritually in public.

In fact, that's all I believe is missing—a right understanding of how to operationalize our principles to build a just peace.

And with this book, my New Thought brother-in-justice does not aim to simply critique our movement, which it does need. But this book was written to assist us with cultivating new understandings for ways we can show up as leaders in this movement, in answer to the call of the times, without abandoning our foundational teachings. This book is a primer. In fact, I consider it required reading for not only New Thought credentialed leaders, but for religious actors from all strata looking for an accessible guide for learning how to move beyond dangerous political neutrality that replicates the violences to which we are principally opposed and for gaining new on-ramps for becoming fully aligned leaders building socially relevant, transformative, 21st century ministries and movements.

And when I say this book is required reading, that's because it is. I now include it in the reading list of the Reading and Research Course that I have the privilege of offering at Harvard Divinity School, called "Camp Courage Academy: A Social Change Curriculum for Credentialed Leaders." Like David, I refuse to be a mere glorified problem-stater or a color-blind spiritual bypasser. When I sing, "Let there be peace on Earth and let it begin with me," I create a curriculum at Harvard to teach about it, and David writes books about it.

I can't wait to see what you will do after reading and applying the wisdom found in *Freedom from Discord.*

– Rev. Dr. Kevin Kitrell Ross
Ordained Unity Minister,
Unity of Sacramento International Spiritual Center

PREFACE

Our world is dangerously polarized at a time when humanity is more closely interconnected—politically, economically, and electronically—than ever before. If we are to meet the challenge of our times and create a global society where all peoples can live together in peace and mutual respect, we need to assess our situation accurately. We cannot afford oversimplified assumptions about the nature of religion or its role in the world.

— *Karen Armstrong,*
Fields of Blood: Religion and the History of Violence

Over the course of my time in pulpit ministry, which began in 2004, I sat down to start writing a book on at least a dozen occasions, maybe more. I struggled in all the ways that most struggle—finding the time, getting distracted, becoming discouraged, or being disoriented from the idea I started with. Every so often, in the process of my research, I came across another book that seemed to capture what I wanted to express. When that happened, I often felt relieved. Thank God, someone else did it. And then the process would start all over.

And still, what I know is that if we listen deeply enough, we each have a unique voice to lend to the world, and as has been said, "There is a book inside of everyone." So, I continued to listen as my ministry unfolded from my start as a youth pastor in a New Thought mega church, to a young, untested founding pastor of a new work, a new church, to a seasoned minister serving in capacities beyond the local pulpit. This book is the result of what I heard from Spirit along the way and what I continue to hear from that still small voice within. It is both a reflection of my ministry and a message to our movement.

I have a lifelong passion for the empowering nature of our teaching, as well as the internal vision and desire to actualize these principles in the world around me in a manner that brings about more peace and justice into our collective experience. I believe every generation of ministers is tasked with contextualizing the teaching and practices of their tradition for their generation and time. And that is where this book comes from.

I grew up in the New Thought tradition, in Religious Science and Science of Mind communities in particular. My mother found the teaching in the early 1980s while in Phoenix. Her first entrée into New Thought was through the Valley of the Sun Church of Religious Science with Rev. Dr. Bob Henderson, whose plaque honoring his many years of service hangs in my office, a gift from his widow, along with his doctoral hood and robe, given to me as a child who grew up in his church.

I grew up during an era of icons, a movement of large, prosperous churches with star-quality ministers who embodied the ethos of "manifest your destiny." Coupled with the mass consumption pace of consumerism in the 1980s and 90s, it seemed a perfect fit, a theological solution to acquiring more good but being spiritually grounded and minded while you do it. What's not to love about that? Well, plenty of things actually, but we will talk more about that as we go.

At the same time, the burgeoning self-help movement started booming. Weekend seminars on finding yourself, exploring your inner child, and learning to create the life you wanted were all the rage. Authors like Wayne Dyer and Deepak Chopra got their start speaking at our churches and selling copies of their first books from the trunks of their cars. It would not be long before self-help gurus filled stadiums. Tony Robinson, Jim Rohn, Les Brown, and Louise Hay were all cashing in on the popularity of the message, and New Thought churches were growing fast.

By the time I entered the ministry in 2004, the landscape already was changing. New churches were not growing at the same rate, and many were already in a slow but visible decline. Over the next twenty years, the New Thought icons of the 1980s and 90s began to fade away, to retirement in most cases. While the level of respect and admiration remained high for each of them, their students clearly did not inherit the same golden age of New Thought. Those who attempted to replicate their success found the shifting sands of time rather than a solid foundation to build on. Retiring ministers bemoaned the warning signs of "church decline" across denominations. Study after study showed the increasing numbers of people with no religious affiliation and un-churched populations, and all the major denominations struggled to capture the next generation.

Studies conducted by Pew Research Center in 2007 and updated in 2019 demonstrate the changing landscape of religious affiliations in the United States. In 2007, 78 percent of Americans identified as Christian, with 16 percent saying they were "religiously unaffiliated." By 2019, 65 percent identified as Christian and 26 percent as unaffiliated or "nones."

Meanwhile, the dawn of the internet generation, smartphones, and social media influenced our social behavior. In his groundbreaking research book, *Bowling Alone,* sociologist Robert Putnam points out that our social capital—time spent interacting with each other in social settings—is in a rapid decline at the dawn of the 21st century. For example, participation in social clubs was down 58 percent; participation in family dinners together, down 43 percent; having friends over, down 35 percent. And these numbers are now more than twenty years old and most certainly have not improved.

The world was changing—and rapidly. Technology that brought greater connectivity also brought greater exposure to areas of our collective human experience we were previously able to ignore, compartmentalize, or simply remain ignorant of. Social media and smart technology meant there was greater sharing of human experiences, from, "Here's what I'm having for dinner," to, "I just witnessed this gross display of sexism, racism, etc.… Here, look!"

Technology seems to demonstrate one of the core principles of New Thought: We are one; we are all connected. The internet seemed proof positive that there really was "one mind" and a collective consciousness we all contribute to and are influenced by. Technology also highlighted the depth of overused platitudes and put a bright spotlight on our personal and collective responsibility to live up to such aspirations. If we are all one, then what are we doing about the inequity being exposed? What do we have say in the face of exposed inequity and injustice?

When Rodney King was beaten by Los Angeles police officers in 1991, the world was able to look on in horror due to a combination of opportune timing, the right equipment (a bulky, shoulder-mounted camcorder), and the moral courage to start filming, knowing the risk of great bodily harm in doing so. Now with body cameras on officers and, more importantly, smartphone cameras with instant recording capacity in the hands of every child, teenager, and adult, we see so much more—more of what has always occurred but is now known to the collective mind (aka, the internet) and to the social conscience of us all. This rise in technology directly contributed to the collective consciousness of humanity and gave us the capacity to measure it in real time via polls, trends, hashtags, and content searches, helping us understand what people are thinking and talking about.

The New Thought movement has a lot to say about collective consciousness, how it's formed, and, more importantly, how to change it. The concept of collective consciousness as it relates to how things work is core to our brand of thinking and teaching.

Yet during the dawn of this online social justice awakening, the New Thought movement and its adherents often remained silent. Conspicuously so. We have not been known as a movement that speaks up and out about social issues. Yet as a licensed and ordained minister in the movement, I found myself regularly polled by friends online and by congregants on Sundays: "Rev., what do you think about this latest exposed injustice in the news? What does our teaching say about that?" Or sometimes more directly: "What does the principle of oneness, or love, or harmony (all tenants of our faith that we call spiritual principles) have to say about that?"

These are excellent questions, questions we ought to ask ourselves and honestly reflect on what the answers expose and express. I call this exploring the radical implication of our teaching/theology. My early sermons were filled with statements like: What is the radical implication of oneness when we experience or witness separation? What is the radical implication of wholeness when we see violent expressions of racism or phobias manifesting as public policy? What then do we say from the lens of our teaching to these moments?

The traditional answer too often had something to do with "individual experience and consciousness of the one experiencing such dis-ease." In other words, if you were not experiencing it directly, then it didn't have much to do with you. Sure, you could pray for the healing of the situation, but it was on "them" to do the work, not me.

Wait, what? This could not be the depth of our teaching, this could not possibly be the radical implication of the tradition I was ordained in and gave a life of service to, could it? Too often it was. And as much as this disturbed me, it also moved me to go deeper, to explore more. I was convinced that these answers were from the shallow end of the pool, that there were deeper waters to explore. So I swam out, far from the safe shores of "I am the author of my experience" and into the turbulent waters of an undifferentiated connection with all humanity.

As a young minister, I frequently meditated on this question: What is my message to the world? What do I have to say in the midst of the time I am living? It was clear to me that I could no longer afford to simply claim my "oneness with everything" while the polarization of American culture raged on, as exposed in our social media feeds. It was time to turn our face outward, face the world of conditions, and speak our message. I was not alone. I felt the turn taking place in our New Thought organizations as well.

By no means am I the sole expert on racial and social justice from a New Thought perspective. Far from it. The plain truth is I am a cis-gendered heterosexual White male, privileged to use my platform to say what, in numerous instances, others have been saying for a long time. I am simply one who dedicated his life to living the principles and seeking to make them real for the places we find ourselves. In writing this book, I am doing what I have always done—living out the truth of my being and faith as I see it. I pray this is one contribution to a growing body of work with many diverse voices.

When I speak of New Thought, I primarily reference my experience of and orientation from a Holmesian perspective and the branch of New Thought known as Centers for Spiritual Living. This, however, should not keep anyone from applying the insights and principles herein to the broader New Thought movement, including my spiritual siblings in the Unity movement, Divine Science, Universal Foundation for Better Living, Affiliated New Thought Network, and International New Thought Association. In fact, in many cases the more Biblical and Christian orientation of both Unity and Universal Foundation for Better Living ought to lead these movements to more readily embrace the principles of a New Thought social justice and liberation theology lens. For those very same reasons, Unity, in particular, may find that the quagmire of upholding White Protestant Christian practices serves as an additional roadblock to the evolution this moment calls for.

In 2005, Centers for Spiritual Living (CSL) embraced a global heart vision, the emerging focus on justice issues within the collective consciousness, and the need for New Thought to be responsive and adaptive to this reality. Both of the major branches of New Thought, Unity and Religious Science, embraced mission statements or guiding documents that included language that took us out of navel-gazing individualism and into global connection; to "make the world a better place" to "create a world that works for everyone" and to "awaken humanity to its spiritual magnificence."

Some, like me, embraced the challenge to articulate our teaching in a manner that met the need in this hour. Others clung to tradition, staying firmly anchored in what they were taught—namely, that it was not our job to be engaged in the "effects" of humanity by fretting over external "conditions" but rather to respond to the noise of the external with an "inner conviction of truth." I even heard a keynote speaker at a major conference proclaim, "The world already does work for everyone, according to their own consciousness." It was difficult for me to sit through that address without gasping aloud at the amount of privilege it takes to make such a claim. Yet, most did not gasp at this line; they applauded as this was the party line in my tradition.

Yet Ernest Holmes, one of the great luminaries of the New Thought movement, reminds us that evolution is the mandate of the universe. Grow or die, he insisted. In particular, he expected that his own movement and body of work would continue to evolve, grow, and expand beyond what he had the time and privilege to articulate.

If you've ever taken the London Underground, you'll remember the frequent reminders in print and audio announcements to "mind the gap." And here we stand, faced with this all-consuming choice, the gap between what we have been and what we could be.

It became clear that as we evolve and continue to contextualize the teachings we hold dear to the age we find ourselves in, that new works, theological reflections, and evolutionary expressions of our ancient wisdom were necessary. As I increasingly considered the implication of New Thought teachings in the current world context, where social justice issues were more and more in the public and traditional and social media spheres, I found myself digging deeper into the principles of New Thought and their profound truth and capacity to meet the call of this moment in a unique way. I was excited by this and by the early 2000s, after establishing my ministry and first pulpit in Portland, Oregon, I began to weave my findings into my messages, teaching, and sermons.

However, much to my great surprise, I was not always met with cheers and accolades for my fresh new thoughts within New Thought. In fact, I was questioned and challenged, sometimes openly by my own congregants and colleagues alike. I was told I was "too focused on the conditions," "too divisive in my choice of words," and "taking the teaching away from its core purpose (namely individual enlightenment)." I was admonished that, "We teach people how to think, not what to think. Teach the principles, and let people form their own opinions about the world and what to do about it." Moreover, I was told my job on Sunday was to bring no offense to anyone, since we are all one. "Oh, is that what that means?" I thought. "Because we are all one, we can't talk about difficult things?" To entertain such a standard immediately reduces our communities to mere social clubs of like-minded souls who enjoy confirming their spiritual leanings rather than belonging to a space that actually grows and challenges them. Hard as it is to admit, I've discovered more people along the journey of my career who prefer the former rather than the latter.

One particularly forceful form of admonishment came after I placed a "Black Lives Matter" sign outside our church, which happened to be situated in a wealthy, White, mostly private enclave of Portland. The sign, like my sermons at the time, was a clear and visible (and audible) demonstration of support and affirmation for the growing movement that sought to bring awareness, justice, and visibility to the brutal attack on Black and Brown bodies by police officers across the United States. I spoke clearly and forcefully to the affirmative statement (a spiritual tool in

New Thought) "Black Lives Matter" as a productive use of our collective consciousness, which when focused with intention will bring about the desire of our affirmation. This, to my mind at least, was pure principle in action—a demonstration of our confessed faith, not a political act that would disturb the pews. I've since learned that often these two things cannot be separated.

But few other New Thought churches were doing so at the time, some in fact were being told directly by their boards or senior leadership to stay clear of using the phrase for fear of offending any congregants. It should be noted here that the vast majority of New Thought churches have predominately White congregations. But capitulating to the potential sensitivities of my congregants was not a skill I had or desired to cultivate (not for a lack of trying by some of my mentors over the years). I did not do this with Easter or Christmas, despite the many sensitivities around such Christian markers that New Thought congregants (more so in CSL than Unity) tended to have. We put on large and powerful "high church" services, complete with organs, robes, lots of candles, and, of course, a metaphysical message, after which I was greeted with congregants' gratitude for "giving them Easter/Christmas back" in a way healed their hearts, because I used New Thought principles to heal the wounds and sensitivities.

The founder of my tradition, Ernest Holmes, was clear: A minister's job is twofold: "To teach and to heal; to heal and to teach. That is it." As such, when someone presents a wound, we can teach the greater truth, and/or we can heal the source of the wound. Among those options is not tiptoeing around the wound so that the infected is never offended, yet often that is the standard that ministers are held to.

And so, as it related to the fractured collective consciousness of race relations in our nation, I took the same principled approach: to teach and heal. I thought this was simple and straightforward, not radical or dangerous. But rather that being greeted with tears of gratitude, I was instead dragged into a meeting with the vice president of our board and our executive director, where I was told, in relation to speaking about Black Lives Matter, "It's not that we disagree with you, Rev. David, but we are hearing from lots of people [always a dangerous phrase], and we are just tired of having to hear it so often." When I say that my response to this was stunned silence, I'm in no way exaggerating. I was unable to form a response. That is, until my tears began to flow, and I said, "I know. I'm tired of having to say it." With that, the meeting ended, but my conviction only deepened.

None of these rebukes, no matter how coded or aggressive they were, sat well with my soul. I knew I had been placed where I was for a specific reason. The calling on my life and message from Spirit was clear and, for better or worse, indifferent to the response I received from others. One of the markings of a true calling, I believe, is that it does not come with the condition, "but only if people like it."

This book is my contribution to that call.

CHAPTER ONE

WHY ARE WE HERE?

FINDING PURPOSE: THE POWER OF STORY

As we begin our exploration of the promise and future of New Thought, we start by grounding ourselves in purpose. What is the purpose of religion or spirituality? What purpose or meaning does New Thought bring to that realm? What is the story we tell about our past, present, and future? Answering these questions is critical to understanding where we are going and how we will get there.

Everything in the universe has purpose because Intelligence created it on purpose. This is true for us as individuals and as communities. And it is true for the systems and structures we create, such as religion and spiritual practices. In this chapter, we explore the meaning and purpose of religion, spirituality, and New Thought as a means of orienting our story and establishing a new one.

If New Thought is to claim a space among liberation theologies of the 21st century, it will require examining deeply who we are, who we want to be, and getting honest about who we have been in the recent past. We will have to get honest about how the systems and structures of capitalism, Whiteness, and patriarchy (among others) have infected and affected the ways and means by which our teaching has been expressed. In other words, the first place to liberate will be our own consciousness and organizations. I believe this work is critical to reclaiming our prophetic zeal that grew our movement in the 1950s through the 1990s. But make no mistake, this is not an attempt on my part to return to the good old days. Rather, my commitment is to point the movement in a bold new direction that both matches the historical moment we find ourselves in and lives up to the promise our teaching provides to change the world through the laws of consciousness.

Bold new directions require critical self-reflection and honest evaluation of the past habits and patterns that get in our way. New Thought communities teach individuals about this process all the time. In a prosperity class, for example, if someone is ready to claim their authority as a prosperous being available to all the good of the universe, we remind them that affirmations alone will not suffice. They must confront all the old beliefs of lack and limitation that get triggered along the way and be willing to uproot and replace them. The same is true for our collective experience as a movement. Old beliefs of political neutrality and silence in the face of overt oppression of those we are inextricably one with will not do. We will have to lean into our affirmations of oneness in ways that push us beyond our comfort zone and keep us ever leaning into our vision. Like everything we teach in the consciousness and mindfulness movement, this begins with the story we tell ourselves about who we are and why we are here.

There is an old Jewish tale that goes something like this: Once there was a man who took long evening strolls after dinner to clear his mind. After one difficult day, he wandered a bit further than usual. He quickly realized he was not familiar with the landscape around him, yet it did his mind good to explore, so he kept walking. Suddenly, he found himself approaching a clearing of trees, and as he emerged, he found himself facing a great wall, tall and stretching as far as the eye could see. At one end, there was a gate and a tower next to it. As he approached in curiosity, he heard a voice from the tower: "Who are you, and why are you here?"

The old man thought for a moment. Having never seen this wall, gate, or tower before, he thought maybe he should be the one asking the questions. While he paused, the voice said again, "Who are you, and why are you here?"

The old man thought of the question even more deeply this time, then a smile moved across his face. He replied, "How much are they paying you?"

"What!" said the man in the tower.

"I said, how much are they paying you?" the old man quickly shouted back.

"What does that have to do with anything? I asked you first. Who are you, and why are you here?"

"Exactly," said the old man. "I'll pay you double to come to my house and ask me that question every day."

Since the dawn of consciousness, the theologies of the world have been seeking to answer this question. Religion and perhaps even the notion of God Itself seems to be born of this question. Who are you, and why are you here? The answer to which is a story passed down from generation to generation.

Story is at the heart of what religion does and is. Religion is a collection of stories about a people and their experiences in the world and how their concept of God did or did not intervene in their time of need or "reward" them in their time of blessing. Often we think of religion or our relationship to it as a form of identity, both individually and collectively. We say, "I am Catholic," rather than, "I practice the Catholic faith." Collectively, religious identity is more simply defined as culture. And if we stop to think about it, 80 percent to 90 percent of what religion actually is can be defined as culture. It is about what to eat and when, what to wear and where, what to do and not do and why, and who we are in relationship to the universe. It's an embodiment of culture that then shapes the community in ways few acknowledge or even see.

Religion fundamentally is the story we tell ourselves about our relationship to God, Creator, The Thing Itself, and each other. As such, it has been an inextricable element in the formation and development of human consciousness from time immemorial. God, or The Thing Itself, as Ernest Holmes called It, is defined by our relationship to It. We don't define The Thing Itself but rather we define our relationship to It through the stories we have about It.

Religious formation traces its roots back some 11,000 years and coincides with our ancestors' shift from a nomadic hunter-gatherer phase to the more sedentary agricultural phase of human existence. This, as it turns out, is the beginning of a crucial thread, which we will see throughout the development and current-day struggles of society and social justice issues. How we settle and make community is at the heart of the issue of justice and how we respond to that which disrupts community standards or expectations.

Think about it: Religion emerges as we take time to sit and converse with each other, often around a meal. Our settling gave way to sharing stories as a means of communing together, which is to say that religion emerges as we begin to tell stories about the universe we live in, its mysteries and meanings, and our relationship to it and to each other. In many ways, not much has changed since then. Religion is the shared story of our experience with the universe, and that story is always evolving. This rather simplistic definition turns out to be vitally important as we move forward.

Years ago, I was in a conference with many great religious scholars and teachers from different denominations, Biblical scholar Dr. Will Coleman was teaching. We were reading from Genesis, and as a group, we got to the third line read out loud, "and God said... ." Dr. Coleman interrupted us: "STOP!" Shocked, we stopped our reading, and we all thought the same thing, "Gee, we did not get very far; we were just starting." Dr. Coleman then asked us, "Who said that God said?" Puzzled, we said, "The text says so." "OK," he responded, "the text says so, Who wrote the text? Whose hand gave God a voice? And did you notice that God did not get a voice until the third verse?"

So here we had what some consider God's infallible, inerrant word, and God does not have a voice until the author gives God one. The point he was making is that religion is nothing more than a collection of stories that humans write about God. And as such, the author of the story has tremendous power to shape how the story is told.

Now at this point, you may say, "Yeah, but the stories are antiquated and religion is a thing of the past." However, antiquated stories simply beg the creation of new ones, and while organized religion continues to shift and change with time, the function remains the same. You see, one of the concepts we will need to liberate ourselves from as we progress on this journey is our misconception of religion itself.

Contrary to popular belief (even among well-respected colleagues in New Thought), religion is not antiquated. It is central to our existence in community for the simple fact that making meaning or sense out of our existence is central to our being. That said, we are evolutionary beings and, as such, the stories we tell and even how we tell them must also evolve.

You and I are those authors. We are not dependent on ancient scrolls and manuscripts pieced together and translated by people living in a completely different world, as the time period represented in the texts demonstrates. We are the authors of our own experiences. We are the contributors to the stories of our time. We are the epistle authors of a 21st century understanding of the relationship between the Divine and its creation.

And while there are many who prefer spirituality over religion, a rapidly growing number of people, that fact really doesn't change the point. After all, what is spirituality but one's personal story of the relationship between self and the universe in which they find themselves? Gather a group of people who share a similar story in their spiritual journey, and a more formal religion is bound to emerge. It's what we do as human beings. Karen Armstrong makes the case in the introduction of her work *Fields of Blood*:

> *In the West we see "religion" as a coherent system of obligatory beliefs, institutions, and rituals, centering on a supernatural God, whose practice is essentially private and hermetically sealed off from all "secular" activities.*

Yet this is simply not the case, as she goes on to prove:

> *But words in other languages that we translate as "religion" almost invariably refer to something larger, vaguer, and more encompassing.*

In fact, what they point to is an integrated systemic way of thinking, behaving, and interacting with the world that can't be isolated or walled off from how we interact with each other and the community we create together. In other words, religion is a much bigger concept and way of life than we've made it in Western societies.

The Arabic "din" signifies as entire way of life. The Sanskrit "dharma" is also a "total" concept, untranslatable, which covers law, justice, morals, and social life.

What is that larger concept? If all societies have religion, as Frans de Waal, a Dutch primatologist and ethologist who studies primate social behavior, pointed out, then what is the social role that it plays? One of the major themes we see in the answer to that question is the role of defining, protecting, and upholding societal structures of justice.

The real role of religion in the work for justice lies in the power of story. Religion, at its base, gives a contextual framework to a people's identity. And that framing story goes a long way to determining whether the contribution to peace and justice is positive or negative. In other words, both religion as a cultural force as well as a personal identity determine our approach to the concept of justice, as well as the efforts to maintain, promote, and share it in the society.

The story we tell ourselves about the essential aspects of life goes a long way in framing how those essential aspects not only influence our own experience but also those of our neighbors, our children, and our future generations. A "framing story," as evangelical author Brian D. McLaren calls it in *Everything Must Change*, is the most essential offering religion can make to the world we create. In fact, McLaren names the lack of an adequate framing story from the world's religions that is capable of healing or deducing the security, equity, and prosperity crisis (respectively) we face as a spiritual crisis and as the leverage point for healing the other major crises we confront.

By "framing story," McLaren means a story that gives people direction, values, vision, and instruction on how to treat one another and how to participate in societies' systems. In New Thought, we call that a "collective consciousness." As individuals and as societies, we are made up of framing stories. They guide, for better or worse, our politics, our justice system, our educational standards, and our personal lives and identities.

THE EFFECTS OF A FRAMING STORY

McLaren offers this explanation of the effects of a framing story:

If our framing story tells us that we humans are godlike beings with godlike privileges—intelligent and virtuous creatures outside a limited environment of time and space, without potentially fatal flaws—we will have no reason to acknowledge or live within limits, whether moral or ecological. Similarly, if it tells us that the purpose of life is for individuals or nations to accumulate an abundance of possessions and to experience the maximum amount of pleasure during the maximum number of minutes of our short lives, then we sill have little reason to manage our consumption. If our framing story tells us that we are in a life-and-death competition with each other, and only the fittest will survive, then each species and group is in a violent struggle to outcompete and gain independence and safety from dominance over all others, then we will have little reason to seek reconciliation and collaboration and nonviolent resolutions to our conflicts. If it tells us that we are simply masses of atoms in a complex and ultimately meaningless fermentation and decay process, that there is no ultimate purpose to existence, no higher value to the story, then we will have little reason to seek transcendence. But if our framing story tells us that we are free and responsible creatures in a creation made by a good, wise, and loving God, and that our Creator wants us to pursue virtue, collaboration, peace and justice, and mutual care for one another, then our society will take a radically different direction, and our world will become a very different place.

Religion has used its power of story to frame how people see themselves, how they feel about their gender, sexual identity, and race. Religious framing stories fueled the Inquisition, the westward expansion of the United States, the Civil Rights Movement, and the infiltration into politics by the religious right. It is religious framing stories, not God Itself, that tell generations of LGBTQIA+ folks that their identities are wrong or immoral or somehow unwelcome. It is religious framing stories that reinforce White Christian nationalism and fuel political culture wars.

The question for New Thought then is what our story will be. By its nature, it can't be merely a variation of the story of our founders. Every generation is tasked with taking the story they inherit and building on it, making it their own, going further while honoring their roots. Do we envision a world that works for everyone, a world of manifested Christ consciousness, a world where love, oneness, and harmony dominate our experiences and expression? And if the answer to that is yes, the most vital question that remains is: What do we offer toward that vision? This question, as answered by our clergy, leadership bodies, practitioners, and members, will determine the course of our teaching.

AUTHORING NEW STORIES

I'd like to propose a model for understanding how we go about authoring this story. It's nothing fancy or even new, but it offers a standard story-building framework that will allow us to contextually hold all the parts in their proper place. You already know what the model is. It is the basic story outline, consisting of three parts: a beginning, a middle, and an end. The beginning is where we place our current status—the world as we see it now, what's in our bank account right now, the status of our relationships, the state of our politics, the environment, everything as it currently is. The end is framed by where we would like to go. It is the vision, the ideal, the kingdom, the "kin-dom," heaven on Earth, a world that works for everyone.

When the end is clear, then the middle, which is the path from here to there, becomes clear. When the destination is set in the GPS, then the path illuminates on the screen before us. However, if it is not clear where we are going, then the path from here to there is murky, varied, and wildly different from person to person.

While it may be a harsh criticism of New Thought to say that our problem or challenge for years was that we did not know where we collectively were going, it may be more accurate to say that we left the answer up to each individual. In other words, individual enlightenment was the destination, and where that was for you would be different for me and for the next person. As a result, there could be no collective path that brought us together, no common cause binding our journey together. The best we could do as a movement was to offer tools via classes and inspirational sermons for the journey: Take what you like and leave the rest. So what is wrong with that? Well, nothing if individual enlightenment is the goal. I am certain that many in our movement would affirm that this is exactly what we should be doing, that it is what makes us unique. Such a response was likely well received 25 years ago, and I am sure endorsed by folks like me (including me).

Yet, as it will be pointed out several times in this book, such an inward and individualistic focus violates our principle of oneness and isolates us from the world and work of care and compassion for our neighbor. Leaning solely on the idea that it is up to individuals to do their own inner work is a position of privilege more than it is a spiritual practice.

What is worse, many in our movement have collapsed the three frames (beginning, middle, and end) into one and then viewed them through a single point. Symptoms of this sound like this: "Consciousness is all there is, and it exists only in a single point of origin, with no past, no future, just the present, in which all needs are already met."

Sure, OK. But tell that to someone struggling to pay the rent, or the person behind you at a red light attempting to get to the hospital because their family member has been in an accident. Their anxiety is boiling over, and you are meditating on the sweetness of the now moment in no hurry to step on the gas when the light turns green because there is no there, only here and now.

Now, it's not that a moment of mindfulness won't help each of these individuals or those in countless other examples we could give. Mindfulness is indeed a powerful practice that can be used in spiritual and justice work alike, as well as, and maybe especially, in gridlock traffic. Yet mindfulness is a moment; it is a practice and a tool to be used in the midst of a lived context. Unless you are a monk who has denounced all worldly possessions and attachments, you live in a world of sequential order, flow, cause and effect, and time (made up as it may be).

If the end point of your story is individualism manifesting personal good, then there really is no reason to read further. Find a spiritual practice that works for you and do it. End of story. But our collective movements and organizations have articulated their visions for the future in terms that suggest otherwise. The depth of our principles and teaching suggest more than a philosophy, which by nature is individualistic. They suggest a theology, which, by its nature, is collective and communal. They suggest collective experience, collective awakening, collective manifestation of prosperity, goodness, and justice for all beings and the planet. A world awakened to its spiritual magnificence must have specificity to it. A world that works for everyone is not an abstract idea but a vision that must be actuated in real everyday terms that can be named, touched, felt, and experienced. To paraphrase Dr. Howard Thurman, you cannot love humanity generically; you must put a name to it.

What then is our framing story in New Thought? Where are we going? Are we a mass of individualized expressions of God, here to learn how to manifest our good through the control of our consciousness, free from the concerns of others or the impact of our individualized quest on them? Or are we one body of consciousness manifesting through individualized points of experience, each inextricably tied to the other in an infinite feedback loop that is intended to evolve, grow, and change as a result of each point of experience, thereby manifesting more good, justice, and peace for all within the One? Is the goal personal enlightenment, where we simply have the life we desire, or is the goal to be emancipated from discord of every nature? And is that goal meant to be attained by all?

In short, it's time to ask the question of ourselves: Who are we, and why are we here? I cannot speak for the movement or any other member, practitioner, clergy, or community, but I can express who I am, as an ordained minister dedicating his life path to this teaching. I can articulate where I am going, in hopes that I will find other sojourners there. I'd like to suggest that our story has a beginning, an ending (that is ever unfolding) or vision, and a middle path that articulates what we need to become and do to manifest the vision. While we each have to author our part, as no one can do it for us, we can also contribute to the collective in a manner that benefits the all.

So why are you here?

I am here to honor a movement grounded in the legacy of our founders' deep roots of consciousness and mystical understanding of universal truths.

I am here to speak the prophetic truth of oneness into a divided world that is still in the grips of racism and White supremacy, in hopes that the clarion call of our divine nature shakes humanity awake.

I am here to affirm the divine potential within all humanity, knowing that our potential is rooted in our responsibility.

I am here to awaken humanity to a magnificence that lives beyond division, yet does not hide from protecting and defending the most vulnerable among us.

I am here to share a generous love ethic that stands in solidarity with those on the margins, without apology.

I am here to participate fully in building a world that works for everyone through the conscious recognition that the means and ways in which current structures do not work for many are upheld by the consciousness behind them and, therefore, must be dismantled through the application of the tools of conscious transformation.

I am here to walk in the radical honesty that is gritty, raw spiritual work that requires shedding the protections of privilege and building authentic relationships with those in the trenches.

I believe New Thought provides a powerful liberative witness to the power within each one of us to radically change the world through personal and collective awakening.

I believe we are created in God's image and are, therefore, the vehicles through which God's wholeness is revealed. The moment we accept this is the moment we must also accept responsibility for any place in the world of effects where that wholeness is not revealing itself.

I believe oneness without responsibility is cheap privilege, because the moment you claim the power of the principle of oneness is the moment you can no longer afford to separate yourself from the pain of the world. That's how oneness works.

I believe the banknote of oneness is cashed in acts of justice.

I believe these convictions can be supported and grounded in the legacy of self-empowering principles found in the New Thought movement. I believe we are built for this moment—but I also believe this moment will require a confrontation with outdated and inadequate practices and beliefs that have held us back from our larger potential and social impact.

APPLYING THE PRINCIPLES

To state it more directly, we, at various levels across the movement, will have to confront several sacred cows that contribute to our current identity and understanding of ourselves. We'll need to confront the lies we've ingested and allowed to have dominion over our experience: Lies that say politics doesn't belong in religion or spirituality. Lies that tell us that church communities are meant to be politically neutral territory, free from culture wars and divisive language. Lies that tell us that conditions of racism, sexism, homophobia, etc., are the result of error thinking by those experiencing or expressing these negative ideas and that all we need to do is not engage or entertain them in our own consciousness. Lies that tell us if we do focus on these negative social conditions, we'll only create more, even if we have good intentions, because we are participating in separation thinking. Lies that keep us safe in the shallow waters of individual experience. Lies that tell us "colorblindness" is a spiritual practice or value.

As we cling to these lies, the law of consciousness can only bring forth the nature of these thoughts, which is isolation, separation, and increasing irrelevance in the midst of a world calling for greater connection, compassion, and collective action. Thus, despite all our efforts in diversity, equity, and inclusion work, training, and language, we can go no further in our experience than our consciousness will allow. Clinging to these lies will not bring more people, resources, or energy to our communities.

We confront these lies and more in these pages, and in particular in Chapter Six. Leading up to this critical examination, we explore the value of story in collective consciousness in Chapter One. In Chapter Two, we examine the impact of violence and justice within stories. In Chapter Three, we explore the rich history and principles of liberation theology as potential grounds for a new story.

With those chapters grounding us, in Chapter Four we take a closer look at the New Thought movement through the lens of liberation theology, Chapter Five offers a review of the history of the movement, unearthing our more radical and justice-oriented beginnings, thereby reframing and reclaiming the story of our past. As mentioned, Chapter Six confronts the lies that stand in the way of stepping into the potential that a liberation theology position affords us. Finally, in Chapter Seven, we look at the vision of what a New Thought Liberation Theology movement would and could look like.

If you've come to the same conclusion I have—that who we've become is no longer working for us—then challenging lies (what we in New Thought refer to as error thinking) is integral to the path of transformation we are calling in. And if we are honest, there is no movement on Earth in a better position than New Thought to understand the complexities as well as the rewards of confronting error thinking, uprooting and replacing it with empowering and affirmed new thoughts that point us in the direction of who we choose to become. This is precisely the work we teach people to do, and it is exactly the work we are called to do now. Our future depends on it.

It is also my opinion that those in the broader progressive liberal Christian movement (including many in the Unitarian Universalist Church, United Church of Christ, Metropolitan Community Church, Unity Fellowship, progressive Pentecostal movement, and beyond) also will find this work applicable and relevant. More and more, we find greater common ground among each other, even as we continue to embrace our unique experiences and worship expressions. Many of these groups are on similar trajectories of branching out beyond the moorings of their denominational harbors and exploring openly the waters of expanded consciousness, radical inclusion, and justice.

It's my observation and a focus of this book that both technology and social consciousness have exposed a moral crisis in our country (and not limited by our borders), a crisis that New Thought and progressive spirituality have an answer for—an answer rooted in a deeper understanding of our oneness, connection, and relationship to one another.

Like the greater construct of theology itself, New Thought was and is a contextual response to the conditions that gave rise to it. It emerged because the conditions were right and the channels (authors and teachers) made themselves available to the moment before them, to brave a new way of thinking and approaching God and spirituality. That was true in the late 1800s when these luminaries first emerged, and it remains true today. And this time, we must avail ourselves of the message that wants to emerge for our time.

Like other major world religions, New Thought makes the attempt to speak a universal language, but no matter how universal a theology or system of religious thought may think that it is, the application of its principles always occurs contextually (that is, within a particular time and space context) by people who also are responding to the world around them. Religions that fail to heed this lesson become dogmatic, irrelevant, and dismissed with the passage of time. Those that are able to keep this wisdom in front of them will find themselves on a trajectory of adaptation, growth, and transformation. I believe New Thought was built for the latter, not destined to be the former.

Evolution is the push of the creative force in and around us that asks us to meet the demands of the moment. We are in the midst of a new wave of social justice and civil rights movement rising up from the collective. We do not need to look far to see the ways in which humanity is seeking freedom, respect, dignity, and emancipated expression. In equal measure, it also is not difficult to see the discord, tension, and oppression of rights playing out in the culture wars around us.

New Thought stands on a proud legacy of self-empowerment in the midst of the public square, but it is both good and right to ask what we bring to the table now. The New Thought movement should not miss the moment before it. A spiritual theology that dares to proclaim a radically inclusive spiritual equality ought to stand up and speak up in a world where basic human rights are denied any of its people. Failure to do so is spiritual maleficence and theologically bankrupt behavior that fails to live up to the principle of Oneness it claims to promote.

So let's get started. ∞

REFLECTION QUESTIONS

1. What is your understanding of the power of story in establishing meaning?

_____

_____

_____

_____

_____

_____

_____

2. Do you think religion, and the story it tells, has had a positive or negative impact on the world?

_____

_____

_____

_____

_____

_____

_____

3. Using the three-stage framework, describe the purpose of New Thought and where it is going in your own words.

_____

_____

_____

_____

_____

4. Describe the purpose of your own path in your words.

_____

_____

_____

_____

_____

5. Where do these two paths cross and intersect? Do they support each other? How?

_____

_____

_____

_____

_____

CHAPTER TWO

RELIGION AND JUSTICE

The Bible I have in front of me has 1,679 pages.
On page eight, the first act of violence occurs. It results
in the first death. Since shortly before this murder occurs,
death is declared to be the punishment for sin, the fact
that the death that follows the first sin is a murder hardly
deserves to be considered merely incidental.
— Gil Bailie, Violence Unveiled: Humanity at the Crossroads

THE ROLE OF JUSTICE IN OUR STORY

To read religious history and development is to read a series of tales of power, control, political dominance, war, and vengeance. We read that God is disappointed in "His" creations and their actions, so much so that He decides to wipe them out and start over again—Noah and the great flood, Jonah and the big fish (not actually described as a whale), and so many others. These accounts raise thought-provoking questions about humanity's relationship with God. They reveal as much, if not more, about what humanity thinks about God than they do about what God thinks about humanity. That is to say, they are projections of human consciousness, reflecting our current understanding of our relationship with a Power and Presence greater than we are.

So, why are religious stories so violent?

Throughout history, scholars and theologians have engaged in debates regarding the moral implications of these stories and their relevance to understanding the nature of the Divine. More than reflecting actual history or even the nature of God, what these stories represent is humanity's relationship with the Divine and their own understanding of justice, community, and the role they play in both.

One of the earliest stories in the Old Testament, the tale of Cain and Abel, presents the tragic consequences of jealousy and violence. Cain's anger and envy lead him to murder his brother, Abel, resulting in a rupture in his relationship with both his sibling and God. This story serves as a cautionary tale, highlighting the devastating consequences of unchecked emotions and the importance of cultivating virtuous qualities. The story addresses our awareness of how we respond to our neighbor when things don't go right.

The narrative of the great flood and Noah's Ark illustrates God's response to human "wickedness" and violence. According to the story, God, saddened by humanity's corruption, decides to wipe out all living creatures except Noah and his family, who are instructed to build an ark to survive the flood. While this account likely sought to make sense of an actual cataclysmic event, it also emphasizes the divine mercy in sparing Noah and providing a new beginning for humanity, i.e. the rebuilding of society.

The Exodus story recounts the liberation of the Israelites from Egyptian slavery. In their pursuit of freedom, they empower Moses, as God's messenger, to confront Pharaoh and demand the release of his people. When Pharaoh refuses, a series of ten devastating plagues befall Egypt, leading to the ultimate freedom of the Israelites. This narrative reflects God's intervention in history to deliver the oppressed and demonstrates the profound consequences of human injustice. God, the story tells us, is a God who responds to and seeks justice for His people. This story tells us the history of a people and their relationship to their understanding of God, and it speaks powerfully to notions of belonging and embracing a covenant with a higher power.

The book of Joshua chronicles the Israelites' conquest of Canaan, a violent and often contentious process. The Israelites, under Joshua's leadership, engage in battles and military campaigns to claim the Promised Land. While the conquest raises ethical questions about the use of violence, it also showcases God's faithfulness to his covenant and the fulfillment of divine promises.

So, why are religious stories so violent?

The stories of violence in the Old Testament or Torah invite contemplation on humanity's relationship with God. These narratives serve as mirrors reflecting the multifaceted nature of human existence, exploring themes such as sin, justice, redemption, and divine intervention. They depict both the inherent moral struggles faced by individuals and communities and the profound consequences of human choices. While the violent aspects of these stories can be unsettling, the violence itself is integral to understanding the broader narrative arc of the Old Testament /Torah, a collection of stories from and about a people's journey to freedom and liberation. The stories highlight the complexities of the human condition, including the potential for both righteousness and moral failing. Moreover, they offer valuable lessons on the consequences of violence, jealousy, and disobedience, while emphasizing the importance of virtues such as faith, repentance, and mercy.

So, why are religious stories so violent?

It is not just in the Torah that we see humanity using the power of story to tell of justice, violence, and the moral implications of how we build community. The Bhagavad Gita, a sacred text of Hinduism, is a profound philosophical and spiritual discourse embedded within the Indian epic, The Mahabharata. It presents a compelling narrative that explores the themes of justice and the divine.

The story takes place on the battlefield of Kurukshetra, where two factions of a royal family, the Pandavas and the Kauravas, stand ready for war. Arjuna, a skilled warrior and one of the Pandava princes, is caught in a moral dilemma about fighting against his relatives and beloved ones. Krishna, an incarnation of the Divine, serves as his charioteer and spiritual guide. The Gita delves into the nature of justice and its various dimensions by exploring the tensions in Arjuna's confrontation. Arjuna's moral dilemma raises questions about the righteousness of warfare and the role of duty. Krishna elucidates the concept of "dharma," which encompasses duty, righteousness, and justice. He emphasizes the importance of fulfilling one's duties and upholding justice without attachment to personal desires or outcomes.

The Gita presents justice as a path guided by principles of truth, fairness, and moral responsibility. Krishna's presence in the Gita represents the Divine intervention in human affairs. Through his teachings, Krishna reveals his true nature as the Supreme Being, the ultimate reality behind the universe. He imparts wisdom and guidance to Arjuna, offering profound insights into the nature of existence, the purpose of life, and the interconnectedness of all beings. Krishna's divine manifestation highlights the transcendence of the Divine and Its intimate connection with humanity.

The Gita explores different paths to attain spiritual enlightenment and union with the Divine. Krishna presents three main paths: the path of selfless action (Karma Yoga), the path of devotion and love (Bhakti Yoga), and the path of knowledge and wisdom (Jnana Yoga). These paths emphasize the importance of self-discipline, devotion, and the pursuit of knowledge in realizing one's true nature and establishing a harmonious relationship with the Divine.

The Bhagavad Gita stands as a profound story of justice and the Divine, offering timeless wisdom and spiritual insights. It presents justice as a multifaceted concept that extends beyond societal norms and encompasses individual moral responsibility. The Gita's teachings emphasize the importance of fulfilling one's duties and upholding righteousness, while recognizing the transcendental nature of the Divine. Through the divine manifestation of Krishna, the Gita conveys the interconnectedness of humanity and the Divine, encouraging individuals to seek spiritual enlightenment and establish a deep and meaningful relationship with the ultimate Reality.

So, why are religious stories so violent?

The history of religion and justice is long. As we established in Chapter One, religion plays a central role in creating a framing story or worldview that both shapes and influences adherents and observers alike. As we see in the stories shared here, central to any religion's orientation to the world is its definition of justice. Justice is fundamental to the story religion tells because justice is ultimately about how we engage in community, in relationships. Justice is more than a moral framework. It's an insight into the story we tell about fairness, restoration, community, order, and peace. Justice is ultimately about relationship, position, and value in the human condition. Religious frameworks are used to explain God's view of justice, but as with all stories, this is a reflection of the consciousness of the one telling the story. God's view of justice is, in fact, the view of the authors of the story.

The Bible is a human product; it tells us how our religious ancestors saw things, not how God sees things.

— *Marcus J. Borg,*
Convictions: A Manifesto for Progressive Christians

WHAT IS JUSTICE?

Justice is the ethical, philosophical idea that people are to be treated impartially, fairly, properly, and reasonably by both the law and arbiters of the law. It is the idea that the laws themselves exist to ensure that no harm comes to another and that when it does, a remedial action takes place to restore balance in the community. Social justice then is how justice plays out in the collective experience of humanity. It concerns itself with the distribution of wealth, opportunity, and rights and privileges within a given society.

Justice in both Judaism and Christianity (aka Biblical justice) is a major influence in the Western world, with tremendous implications in Western society and the secular judicial system. Justice is the crowning virtue of the Biblical God as creator, as universal ruler, and as protector and savior of those treated unjustly. Therefore, God's chosen Jewish monarchs (literally, messiahs) represent God in the world doing justice, especially for the widow and orphan, and saving people from empires of oppression. This characteristic task of God as king is a common Ancient Near Eastern (ANE) tradition, and it leads us to the story development of prophets in the Hebrew text, used in both Judaism and Christianity. The role of the prophet was literally to "stand in the gap"—that is, the gap that exists between God's word and the experiences of God's people at any given time. The role of the prophet was to remind the social elite that no matter how much power or control they may have held at any one time, God's law was the last word, and any form of oppression to God's people would be rectified in the end.

This understanding of the role of the prophets in relation to religion and justice has led to the prophetic tradition of preaching and justice work within both Christianity and Judaism.

In his seminal work, *Violence and the Sacred,* René Girard argues that it is the role of the religious institutions that mythologize and perpetuate violence into neat categories of sacred and profane that enable the larger society to move through the cycles of formation, destruction, and reformation.

> *Human history is the relentless*
> *chronicle of violence that it is because when*
> *cultures fall apart they fall into violence, and*
> *when they revive themselves they do so violently.*

— *Gil Bailie,* Violence Unveiled: Humanity at a Crossroads

Primitive religion is the institution that remembers the reviving violence mythologically and ritually reenacts its spellbinding climax. Primitive religion raises one form of violence, a moral monopoly, endowing it with enough power and prestige to preempt other forms of violence and restore order. The famous distinction between "sacred" and "profane" is born as the culture glorifies the decisive violence (sacred) that brought an episode of chaotic violence (profane) to and end ... .

— *Gil Bailie,* Violence Unveiled: Humanity at a Crossroads

In other words, it is through the stories we tell, the stories that make warriors into worshipers, that we turn the profane sacred and the unjust holy. The stories we tell tell the story. So how can we exert that religion has any role in the establishment of justice at all?

RELIGION AS PROPHETIC VISION

What we have discussed thus far is the myriad ways in which religion is used as a sacred story to make sense of the past or the history of a people via their relationship over time. Religion can also be a story of the future, a promise yet to unfold. You might envision religion as the sacred

Chart 2.1, "Religion as Prophetic Vision and Sacred Story": Religion holds the sacred space where we make sense of the past as well as articulate what is possible in the future of human history and our relationship with the Divine.

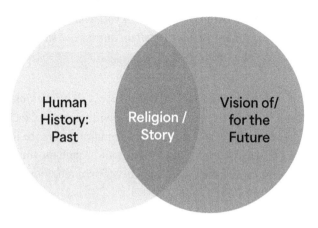

Human
History:
Past

Religion /
Story

Vision of/
for the
Future

space between two conjoining circles, known in mathematics as the Vesica Pisces, with one circle being the unfolding of human history and the other being the vision or promise—and with religion being the sacred center. Interestingly this sacred symbol is found throughout Christianity.

As such, in the same way that religious ideology has been at the heart of violence throughout human history, the same ideology is often at the heart of ending that violence and establishing a new order. Religion and the story it tells is the pulse from which a vision of a better future beats its way into the human heart. Because religion is about the story of our relationship with the Divine, the story always contains the transcendent aspirational element that draws us nearer to a self and to a possibility not yet realized. It is that "angel of our higher nature," as Abraham Lincoln called it, that seeks to live in, through, and as us that serves as the beginning of humanity's justice work. Whether it is through the eight-fold-path of Buddhism or the Sermon on the Mount of Christianity, the transcendent Divine always invites us, as Its instrument, to seek ways of peace, justice, and wholeness in our world and with each other.

*Neither revolution nor reformation can ultimately
change a society, rather you must tell a new powerful tale,
one so persuasive that it sweeps away the old myths
and becomes the preferred story, one so inclusive that
it gathers all the bigs of our past and our present into a coherent
whole, one that even shines some light into the future so
that we can take the next step.... If you want to change
a society, then you have to tell an alternative story.*

— Ivan Illich

We see then that the story we tell, whether we call it religious or not, is critical to both the experience we have as individuals and as society. And if religion, like it or not, is *a* major, if not *the* major, influence in crafting the stories we tell, the stories that influence and shape us, then we need to understand the essential elements of a functional religious storytelling system.

WHAT MAKES A GOOD STORY?

Metaphor is the only language religion has.

— Richard Rhor

The three functions essential to any religion or spiritual orientation to the world are:

1. Use the language of metaphor to tell a story.

2. Create meaning and ritual for the community, often through adherence to faith practices and beliefs.

3. Provide a prophetic voice to guide the community through turbulent times. This happens through both defining and defending the meaning of justice as it relates to the public good and individual practice.

None of these three elements inoculate religion from being abused or corrupted. All religious traditions can fall into the trap of justifying and initiating violence. And by so doing, they make violence sacred. Yet these same functions can be used to enact justice, equality, protection for the marginalized, and hope for a more just and equitable world.

Religion ebbs and flows as it evolves through the hearts and minds of believers entrusted with its sacred role in history and community building. And when religion fails or is found wanting, as it has over and over again throughout history, something transcendent in the human heart perseveres, pushes through, and demands new stories, new meaning, new rituals, and new thoughts to guide the collective forward. I believe that this eternal push is the call for justice, and it is my conviction that this call has been at the heart of the evolutionary push in consciousness behind the emergence of and development in the New Thought movement.

What we see throughout the world's religions is the major role that the theme of justice forms in the structure of thought, story, and moral guidance to society and the people identified with a particular religious practice. Justice shapes the stories we tell. Justice erects the guideposts of right and wrong. Justice tells us how to achieve peace and prosperity, not only as individuals but as communities of people.

Justice as a theme in New Thought is, however, a bit more illusive, at least at the community and society levels. Unlike most of the world's religions, New Thought does not historically take on the articulation of moral codes or community-wide standards imposed on the collective by our understanding of God. Rooted in the belief that individuals have the power to shape their own realities through their thoughts and beliefs, New Thought philosophy views justice as an inherent aspect of divine order. From aligning with universal laws to embracing personal responsibility, justice in New Thought philosophy offers a personal approach to living in harmony with the Divine.

In New Thought philosophy, justice is not seen as an external system of rules or punishments, but as an inner alignment with divine order. The core belief is that there is an underlying intelligence and harmony in the universe, often referred to as God, the Divine, or Universal Mind. Justice, therefore, is understood as the recognition and embodiment of this divine order in our thoughts, beliefs, and actions. By aligning ourselves with universal principles such as love, compassion, and abundance, individuals can experience justice as the natural flow of life, the result, if you will, of their good choices and aligned consciousness. As such, the experience of justice is left to the individual, conditioned on the individual's responsibility to be in alignment in consciousness.

Several additional factors influence the concept of justice within New Thought, including the Law of Mind, the principle of oneness, and the power of thought. The Law of Mind as defined in New Thought is not based on an anthropomorphic Godhead filled with a projected moral vision of culture. Rather, it is an exacting law of nature that responds to what it is given, like the soil responds to the seed implanted in it. Therefore, justice is often thought of as the logical and necessary outcome of the individual's use of the Law of Mind or consciousness.

This use is enacted through the power of thought. Think good thoughts, get good results from the Law of Mind. Think bad thoughts, get bad results from the Law of Mind. The Law of Mind itself does not care. It is just the law. It is just the way it works.

APPLY THE PRINCIPLES TO ACHIEVE JUSTICE

In practice, justice in New Thought philosophy involves consciously applying the principles of alignment with divine order and personal responsibility to everyday life. This can be achieved through various means, including the following.

Conscious creation: New Thought philosophy teaches that individuals are co-creators of their reality. By focusing on positive and life-affirming thoughts and intentions, individuals can contribute to the manifestation of justice in their own lives and in the world. This may involve practicing forgiveness, cultivating compassion, seeking peaceful resolutions to conflicts, and taking responsibility for personal conflict or discord by leaning into the lessons such experiences hold.

Law of attraction: According to the law of attraction, like attracts like. By aligning our thoughts, beliefs, and emotions with justice, we can attract experiences that reflect fairness, equality, and harmony. This principle encourages us to focus on what we desire rather than dwelling on what we perceive as unjust or lacking.

Social responsibility: New Thought emphasizes the importance of personal responsibility in creating a just and harmonious society. This involves taking action to promote positive change, supporting social justice causes, and participating in community service. By embodying justice in our actions, we contribute to the collective transformation and the realization of a more just world. For the most part, social responsibility has been seen as a personal activity rather than a collective moral demand. However, that view has been shifting and changing at various levels throughout New Thought. As communities begin to act together, be it at Pride events, food pantries, coat drives, or other charitable works, we grapple with the question of what our collective moral responsibility is—if we dare to think ourselves as being one with everything and everyone.

While the emphasis on personal responsibility can never be lost or forgotten within a New Thought approach, the more we work with the laws of consciousness at the personal level, the more we realize how consciousness contributes to systems and structures that govern both individual and collective life. These same systems, created and sustained by consciousness, are responsible for societal inequities, injustice, and defamation of the human dignity of those on society's margins. Does our view of social responsibility extend beyond charitable works into advocating for systemic change if those systems are held together by the consciousness behind them and if consciousness is the primary focus in New Thought?

Visioning: Visioning is a spiritual practice, grounded in reflective meditation in which individuals and groups make themselves available to a higher vision that comes from Spirit for a particular cause. This cause could be Spirit moving in their individual lives, a project they are working on, or a group activity. Visioning gives us the opportunity to open up and sense what lies beyond our ego, preference, or desire and capture a higher thought from the Divine Itself. This practice provides the avenue through which the prophetic voice of Spirit can speak in our lives.

A prophetic voice is always a voice that calls us beyond current circumstances into the vision of a greater good. It is a voice that reminds us that we are not bound by current circumstances and that systems and structures of inequity have no power to limit the move of Spirit, which is always seeking to liberate Its creation into its fullest expression, unencumbered and free. If through visioning we sense and see a world that works for everyone, what then is our responsibility in manifesting said vision through our actions and behaviors?

While New Thought historically may not be familiar with the "prophetic voice" tradition, it nonetheless includes the presence of one, which is to say, it has a moral vision of what the world could be. This prophetic voice lives in the guiding visionary documents such as the Global Vision for Centers for Spiritual Living (Appendix C) and Unity's Statement of Social Action (Appendix D). The fullness of the Divine within humanity actualizes these visions. New Thought teachings claim to provide the tools to bridge the gap between here and there.

Similarly, liberation theologies, as we will begin to explore in the next chapter, proclaim a vision of the liberated state of humanity and seek to be a guiding force for humanity in the journey to fulfill that vision. All liberation theologies are systemic responses to social injustice that emerge from prophetic tradition. In other words, liberation theology is the byproduct of a prophetic tradition seeking to address (in a systemic way) the injustices of the world.

The question is whether New Thought is a liberative response. I would argue that the answer to that question rests entirely on the framing story we give to New Thought as a movement. Regardless of whether or not it has been thought of in this way in the past, it can and, in my opinion, ought to be framed this way now. I believe it must be, if it is to survive the cycle of radical reordering we find ourselves in. ∞

1. Why do you think there is so much violence present in religious history and stories?

_____

_____

_____

_____

_____

_____

_____

2. Why is justice an important theme of religious stories?

_____

_____

_____

_____

_____

_____

_____

3. What are the three functions of religion?

_____

_____

_____

_____

_____

_____

_____

4. How does New Thought define justice?

_____

_____

_____

_____

_____

_____

_____

CHAPTER THREE

LIBERATION THEOLOGY

*Theology is contextual language—that is, defied by the human
situation that gives birth to it. No one can write theology for all
times, places, and persons.*

— James Cone,
For My People: Black Theology and the Black Church

PRINCIPLES AND PRACTICES THAT
DEFINE LIBERATION THEOLOGY

Those familiar with the term liberation theology likely have one of
two primary points of contact: Catholic/Latin liberation theology or
Black liberation theology, both of which are historically appropriate
origin points that we will explore in more depth. Liberation theology
as it stands today is a category unto itself in the religious landscape,
with several distinct sub-classifications such as Black liberation, Latinix,
Queer, Feminist, Womanist, Native American, and Asian American.

Interestingly, the emergence and defined borders of one seem to give
rise to the next and, thus, collectively represent an emergence of a steady
stream of expanding consciousness widening its circle of inclusivity. Liberation theology, when studied in its full context, can be viewed as an
ever-expanding and contextualized experience of theology.

Each of these variations of liberation theology contextualize a particular community that the theology seeks to serve. In this way, there seems
to be room for an ever-increasing number of variations, as the principles
of applied liberation theology, which we will review, are embraced by a
unique subset of the diverse community of God's creation.

Meanwhile, a thread of common principles can be seen and studied as we become familiar with the varied expressions. Indeed, the very presence of so many expressions of liberation theology gives rise to the question: Is there a universal set of liberation theology principles? I believe the answer to that question is yes.

It is my aim to lay out these principles as we explore the variations, in much the same way that New Thought represents the common thread among various spiritual traditions and seeks to apply that common thread to the universal desire of humanity to know itself.

SOME HISTORICAL CONTEXT

Liberation theology first emerged in the late 20th century in Latin America and then in the United States. Today's liberation theology movement includes as many as half a dozen main branches, each with further diversification among them and all following a distinct pattern in their emergence, which further bolsters the claim for New Thought to be included among them.

Before we venture too far down that road, let's review some of the core branches of the movement and their unique contributions.

Gustavo Gutiérrez, a Peruvian Catholic theologian, is widely recognized as the father of liberation theology, specifically Catholic liberation theology. Steeped in the context of Latin America's social and political struggles, Gutiérrez developed a theological framework that integrates faith and action, advocating for the liberation of the oppressed and marginalized. Gutiérrez's key ideas and contributions to liberation theology focus on the intersection of faith, justice, and social transformation.

In the 1960s and 1970s—when Latin America faced widespread poverty, economic inequality, political oppression, and human rights abuses—Gutiérrez saw the need for a transformative response from his Catholic practice. Inspired by the Second Vatican Council's call for social justice, Gutiérrez developed liberation theology as a response to these systemic injustices.

Central to Gutiérrez's thought is the notion of what he called "God's preferential treatment for the poor." He argues that because God has a special concern for the poor and marginalized, theology should be grounded in their struggles for liberation. Gutiérrez contends that faith should not be separated from social and political realities. Instead, it should be an active force in transforming unjust structures and promoting more just and equitable societies.

Liberation theology proposes a holistic approach to faith, emphasizing praxis—the integration of theory and action. Gutiérrez highlights the need for critical reflection on sociopolitical conditions, coupled with concrete efforts to address systemic injustices. He believes that faith, when lived authentically, compels individuals to engage in collective action to challenge oppressive structures and work toward a society that upholds dignity, equality, and justice for all.

BLACK LIBERATION THEOLOGY

Black liberation theology is most commonly associated with its most prolific designer, theologian James Cone. Cone's work emerged in 1970 without his having a prior awareness of Gutierrez's work in Latin America. Cone responded to the contextual framework of his experience, in which the tensions between Black theology (What does it mean to be Black and Christian?) and Black liberation (Does Christianity free or hurt Black Americans?). In his work *For My People: Black Theology and the Black Church,* Cone wrote that his efforts "represented the theological reflections of radical Black clergy seeking to interpret the meaning of God's liberating presence in a society where Blacks were being economically exploited and politically marginalized because of their skin color."

In other words, Cone's Black liberation theology addressed the question: What does it mean to be Black and Christian in America, where Black people were oppressed and mistreated?

The Black theologian must reject any conception of God which stifles Black self-determination by picturing God as a God of all peoples. Either God is identified with the oppressed to the point that their experience becomes God's experience, or God is a God of racism... . The blackness of God means that God has made the oppressed condition God's own condition. This is the essence of the Biblical revelation. By electing Israelite slaves as the people of God and by becoming the Oppressed One in Jesus Christ, the human race is made to understand that God is known where human beings experience humiliation and suffering. ... Liberation is not an afterthought, but the very essence of divine activity.

— *James Cone,* A Black Theology of Liberation

Cone lays out the origin of Black theology, which he says arises from three major contexts:

1. The Civil Rights Movement of the 1950s and 1960s

2. The publication of *Black Religion* by Joseph Washington in 1964

3. The rise of the Black Power Movement, influenced by Malcolm X's philosophy

He writes, "From the beginning, Black theology was understood by its creators as Christian theological reflection upon the Black struggle for justice and liberation … ."

This desire by Black theologians to understand the pressing realities of the Black experience in the United States was amplified by the fact that the great majority of White churches (and White theologians) denied any relationship between the Black experience and Christianity. They further claimed that "religion and politics do not mix"—a hallmark identifier of privileged White Protestant theology.

To make matters worse, the White Christian community expected the racial integration of society to lead to Black assimilation within Christianity, an assimilation that would erase the need to focus on the Black experience in the United States. In 1964, Black scholar Joseph Washington's book, *Black Religion: The Negro and Christianity in the United States,* made the claim that there was a unique expression of Black religion distinct from any other form of Protestantism or any other form of Euro-American Christianity. However, he claimed that because this unique expression was denied acceptance within mainstream Christianity, the expression was not genuine Christianity. As a result, he concluded, the Black community only had "folk religion" and "folk theology." His work was widely accepted in White spaces and by White scholars because it helped them in their desire to dismiss and diminish the Black experience, as well as the contribution that was being made to Christianity itself by Black theology. While his work acknowledged the uniqueness of the Black experience in religion, it also gave White communities and scholars a reason to reject the Black experience.

In large part, Black theology was created by Black clergy to refute the two main claims of Washington's work: 1.) that Black religion is not Christian, and 2.) that the Christian gospel has nothing to do with the struggle for justice in society.

The Black Power Movement arose out of the activist work of Stokely Carmichael, Malcom X, and others, in a concerted effort to empower the voices and experiences of the Black Americans and their communities. When community activists began separating themselves from the commitment to nonviolence, White Christian communities urged them to denounce Black Power as "dangerous and unChristian." They refused, and the National Committee of Negro Churchmen organized conferences nationwide and published its "Black Power Statement" in 1966.

> *The Black Power Statement represents*
> *the beginning of a radical theological movement*
> *toward the development of an independent*
> *black perspective on the Christian faith.*
>
> — *James Cone,*
> For My People: Black Theology and the Black Church

It was becoming clear, as Cone delineates, that a theology created for "comfortable White suburbia could not answer questions that Blacks were asking in their struggle for dignity in the wretched conditions of the riot-torn ghettos of U.S. cities." The Black Power Movement represented the end of White-Black Christian coalition building seeking change through nonviolence. In short, The National Committee of Negro Churchmen was making the claim that White Christianity and the theology that justified it was morally bankrupt and found wanting. It was the inadequate response of mainline Christian communities that gave rise to the need for a liberation theology for and by the Black community.

We will see how this state of inadequate response by the dominant group is a major indicator of conditions that give rise to liberation theologies in general.

At the heart of Black liberation theology is the conviction that God is on the side of the oppressed and that the Divine's message holds a special significance for those suffering from racial injustice. It challenges traditional interpretations of Christianity that perpetuated the subjugation and marginalization of Black people. Black liberation theology proclaims the inherent dignity and worth of all individuals, emphasizing the importance of racial pride, self-determination, and the eradication of systemic racism.

This theology places a strong emphasis on social justice and the dismantling of oppressive structures. It calls for a radical reimagining of society and the redistribution of power and resources. It also recognizes the importance of solidarity and collective action, seeking to build alliances and partnerships with other marginalized communities in the fight against injustice.

In Black liberation theology, salvation is understood as a holistic concept that encompasses both spiritual and social liberation. It rejects a narrow focus on individual salvation and emphasizes the interconnectedness of personal and communal liberation. It advocates for a liberation that addresses the socioeconomic, political, and cultural dimensions of oppression, while recognizing the transformative power of God's love and grace.

Central to Black liberation theology is the image of the Black Christ. This depiction serves as a symbol of identification for African Americans, who have historically been presented with a Eurocentric version of Jesus. The Black Christ represents a God who identifies with the suffering and struggles of the Black community, offering hope, liberation, and the promise of a more just future. This image challenges the dominant narrative and affirms the worth and dignity of Black lives.

DIVERSIFICATION OF LIBERATION THEOLOGY

In the diversification of the forms of liberation theology, we see the pattern emerge, a common thread that runs through each one and, as we will see, frame the principles and characteristics of all forms of liberation theology.

Feminist Liberation Theology: Feminist theology emerged out of critique of James Cones's Black liberation work and the conspicuous absence of female voices. Cone welcomed the critique, just as he saw the door open for the emergence of something new to be birthed in the same way his work had come forth.

Feminist theology critically examines the patriarchal assumptions embedded within religious traditions and theological discourse. It highlights how traditional interpretations of scriptures, religious practices, and hierarchical structures perpetuate the subordination and marginalization of women. By questioning and deconstructing these patriarchal norms, feminist theology seeks to transform religious spaces into inclusive and empowering environments that honor the full humanity of all individuals.

Feminist theology seeks to reclaim and amplify the voices of women within religious narratives, traditions, and leadership roles. It engages in critical Biblical scholarship to uncover the often overlooked stories of women and their contributions to religious history. By highlighting these narratives, feminist theologians, like Valerie Saiving and Mary Daly, aim to challenge the male-centric interpretations and expand the understanding of the Divine, promoting inclusive and egalitarian religious practices and contextualized feminist perspectives.

Feminist theology sees the feminist
struggle for justice as central to its task.
It provides an alternative vision of reality, one in
which justice, mutuality, and compassion prevail.

— *Rosemary Radford Ruether*

*Feminist theology aims to reveal the oppressive
structures and narratives within religious traditions
and to work toward their transformation. It seeks to create a
space where women's experiences are valued, their voices are
heard, and their contributions are recognized.*

— *Elisabeth Schüssler Fiorenza*

Feminist theology seeks to build an inclusive theological framework that recognizes the diverse experiences and contributions of women. It incorporates women's experiences, values women's voices and leadership, and promotes gender equality within religious institutions. By reimagining and reconstructing theological concepts and practices, feminist theology offers a transformative vision that challenges traditional hierarchies, fosters inclusivity, and empowers women and marginalized communities.

Womanist Liberation Theology: Likewise, womanist theology emerged to say that feminists did not take into account the perspectives of Black women. Womanist theology emerged within African American communities and encompasses the experiences and struggles of Black women. It is deeply rooted in the sociocultural and historical contexts of Black women in the United States.

Womanist theology embraces the concept of intersectionality, a term coined by Kimberlé Crenshaw, a Civil Rights activist and legal scholar, recognizing that systems of oppression are interconnected. It acknowledges the need for solidarity and collaboration among different marginalized groups to challenge and dismantle these intersecting systems of oppression. By working in partnership with other liberation movements, womanist theologians strive for a more inclusive and just society that addresses the needs and concerns of all individuals.

Methodist minister Jacquelyn Grant, one of the founders of womanist theology, wrote *White Women's Christ and Black Women's Jesus: Feminist Christology and Womanist Response.* In it Grant examined the ways in which Black women interpret Jesus's message, noting that their experience is not the same as Black men or White women. She argues that contextualizing Jesus from the perspective of Black women brings greater insight into and appreciation for Jesus's liberative message. She pointed out that many Black women must navigate the threefold oppression of racism, sexism, and classism. For Grant, Jesus is a "divine co-sufferer," who suffered in his time like Black women do today.

Queer Liberation Theology: Queer liberation theology explores the experiences of LGBTQIA+ individuals within theological and religious contexts. It challenges heteronormativity, homophobia, and transphobia, and it seeks to create inclusive and affirming spaces for queer individuals. Notable theologians in this field include Marcella Althaus-Reid, Patrick S. Cheng, Nancy E. Pittman, and Bishop Dr. Yvette Flunder.

One of its central tenets is the assertion that God's love is inherently inclusive, embracing all individuals regardless of their sexual orientation or gender identity. This contrasts sharply with traditional interpretations that often stigmatize and marginalize queer individuals.

In Queer Liberation Theology, salvation is not solely about an afterlife but involves the liberation of individuals from societal and religious structures that perpetuate oppression. This liberation is seen as a collective struggle for justice, where the marginalized reclaim their rightful place within religious communities. Embracing the idea of "queer kinship," this theology fosters a sense of belonging and solidarity among LGBTQIA+ individuals who often find themselves on the fringes of mainstream religious institutions

Indigenous Liberation Theology: Indigenous liberation theology centers on the experiences and struggles of Indigenous Peoples globally. It addresses issues such as colonization, land rights, cultural preservation, and self-determination. Indigenous theologians and scholars, such as Aloysius Pieris and Virgilio Elizondo, have contributed to this field. It challenges Eurocentric interpretations of Christianity that often have been used to justify the subjugation of Indigenous cultures. This theology seeks to reclaim and reinterpret Christian teachings in ways that align with Indigenous worldviews, emphasizing the sacredness of all creation.

The relationship between Indigenous Peoples and their ancestral lands is central to Indigenous liberation theology. The theology asserts that the land is not just a physical space but a sacred entity, intricately tied to the identity, spirituality, and well-being of Indigenous communities. The struggle for land rights is therefore inseparable from the broader quest for liberation.

Indigenous liberation theology emphasizes the importance of cultural revitalization as an act of resistance. The preservation of languages, traditions, and artistic expressions becomes a way to assert Indigenous identity in the face of cultural assimilation. This theological framework encourages a holistic understanding of liberation that encompasses spiritual, cultural, and political dimensions.

Asian Liberation Theology: Asian liberation theology emerged in various Asian countries and contexts, including the Philippines, South Korea, and India. It addresses issues such as poverty, imperialism, and social injustice, combining local cultural and religious traditions with the principles of liberation theology. Notable theologians include C.S. Song, Aloysius Pieris, and K. C. Abraham.

Eco-Liberation Theology: Eco-liberation theology focuses on ecological and environmental concerns as integral to liberation. It recognizes the interconnectedness of all creation and calls for ecological justice, sustainable practices, and the protection of the Earth. Eco-theologians like Leonardo Boff and Ivone Gebara have contributed to this field.

PRINCIPLES AND CHARACTERISTICS

What we see in each of these examples is a common condition that gave rise to their formation. In traditional New Thought fashion, we can study the universality of the principles at play in the formation of these theologies and then apply what we learn to our own context.

LIBERATION THEOLOGY IS EMERGENT

The first principle of every form of liberation theology is that it is emergent. These theologies emerge as a response usually to the failure of the dominant and/or predecessor theology to meet the needs of its people, more specifically a marginalized group of people. Gutiérrez's liberation thinking arose out of the inadequate response of the Catholic Church to address the needs of the poor. Black liberation arose out of the Black Power Movement's critique of Christianity. Feminist theology emerged out of Black liberation's exclusion and consideration for the experiences of women. Womanist theology emerges out of the exclusion of Black women's voices in the feminist movement, and so on.

LIBERATION THEOLOGY IS CONTEXTUAL

The second principle of liberation theology is that it is contextual. It is anchored in the experience (context) of a group of people, who once again view the dominant theological system as being inadequate in the task of speaking to their struggle or context of their experience and marginalized status within the culture. This is evident in the descriptors of each nuanced version of liberation theology as expressed in their names. (Black, Women, Feminist, Latinx, etc.). Each of these descriptors define the experiential context that the theology addresses and who it is for.

LIBERATION THEOLOGY IS THE BYPRODUCT OF CONTEXTUALIZING THEOLOGICAL PRAXIS

The third principle we see in liberation theologies is that the theology itself is a result of a contextualization of theological praxis (or practice). Put more plainly, liberation theologies are the result of exploring the radical implications of the overarching faith system. These theologies exist as a result of the attempt to contextualize the gospel (good news) in relationship to and for the marginalized—not in theory but in real time. Some might call it "putting it to work."

This principle is extremely important to understand. It states that each theology is not seeking to debunk its predecessor, but rather to radically live out the truth hidden within it. Very often the authors do not or did not seek to establish new religions or sects, but rather they sought to apply the principles of their base religious expression to the specific needs of their people and communities.

THE LIBERATION THEOLOGY PERSPECTIVE

Together, these three principles (emergence, context, and praxis) help shape and guide the evolution of what becomes known as a liberation theology perspective. But that is not all. These theologies can also be studied for the common characteristics operating within them.

Whereas principles help shape the evolution of a liberation theology, the characteristics are what helps define how they operate. Put another way, principles deal with the context in which the theology arises, and characteristics deal with the content and how it operates.

Liberation theologies are defined by the following common characteristics:

1. Solidarity with the oppressed
2. Lifting up of the oppressed
3. Uniting with a liberating force
4. Being political in nature but religious in commitment

First, solidarity with the oppressed or margnalized is shaped by the first principle, which deals with emergence and helps define who the intended audience is. That is to say, because the theology is emergent from a lack of adequate response by the dominant religious identity, its main characteristic is solidarity with the audience it has identified as being on "the margins." For Gutiérrez, "God sides with the poor"; for James Cone, "Jesus is Black"; and so on. The idea that both God and Jesus are for the empowerment and uplifting of the poor in liberation theology is specific. This emphasis is meant to disturb and motivate those who hear it. Namely, if I consider myself Christian and am anything other than poor, then I, too, must also be an advocate for the poor and a champion of economic justice. As liberation theology diversified, the definitin of "poor" expanded or was replaced with various oppressed states of existence.

Second, affirmation that the oppressed state is not the God-ordained or natural state of their group, shaped by principle two, which deals with context. Speaking the faith into the experience of a particular audience means applying the highest ideals of the theology to the identity of the people and their community directly. Here we see the theology take shape to say that because God is for and with you, your state of oppression or marginalization is neither fixed nor the intention of the Divine for your life.

Third, liberation theologies seek to unite the people they serve with a liberating force found in the praxis of their faith, thereby making the state of liberation, rather than the status of salvation, the goal of the faith. This characteristic is shaped by principle three (praxis), which seeks to apply the implications of the faith to its farthest reach at the intersection of its audience. The focus of the faith, therefore, is no longer about theories of the afterlife or the number of angels on the head of a pin, but rather the changed and transformed lives of those living in the faith. In short, the focus becomes living the kingdom rather than fantasizing about it. As the focus shifts from earning status in the sweet by and by to living out the kingdom or promise of God here and now, justice work comes into focus and provides the means to the ends. That is, if we are to live the kingdom now, we must demonstrate that we know what it is and help ensure others can access it as well.

Finally, liberation theologies are political in nature and religious in commitment. This final common characteristic gets the most attention and is the one on which many would seek to dismiss the association between New Thought and liberation theology. But denying the connection would be a mistake and would demonstrate only a surface understanding of both New Thought and liberation theology.

To better understand this characteristic, we need to understand its elements. To be political in the 21st century has become an accusation charged with strong emotions and judgments, not to mention a space most White Protestant churches seek to avoid. But by pure definition, to be political is to be concerned with the activities that govern our collective social experience. A liberation theology by definition must be political in nature because the society in which it operates chooses to make political the bodies, lives, and conditions of the people for whom the theology exists. In other words, the politicizing of women, African Americans, LGBTQIA+, poor people, health care, marriage, etc., demands the theology formulate a response anchored in the tenants of the faith.

While this naturally leads to social justice activities and, therefore, political action in these communities, remember that these actions are anchored in a religious commitment. That commitment is the radical experience of living the demands of the faith. Thus, the goal is the embodied and demonstrated experience of the spiritual and religious truths held by the faith tradition. Political actions per se are a means to an ends, not the ends in themselves. This point cannot be emphasized enough because the political action grabs the attention, both internally and externally. This attention leads to the accompanying critique, carrying both positive and negative consequences, that the faith tradition is solely about said political action, typically of one side or the other of the political aisle.

However, when properly understood, we see that living the principles of the faith is always the goal. And where the expression of that falls on the political spectrum is, at most, secondary if not immaterial all together to the practice of the faith. Properly understood, this both galvanizes and clarifies the faith of the community. ∞

1. Have you previously encountered liberation theology? In what context?

_____

_____

_____

_____

_____

_____

_____

2. In your own words, how would you define liberation theology?

_____

_____

_____

_____

_____

_____

_____

_____

3. What are the principles and characteristics of liberation theologies? How do you see them relating to your experience of faith?

_____

_____

_____

_____

_____

_____

_____

_____

_____

_____

_____

_____

_____

_____

_____

_____

CHAPTER FOUR

NEW THOUGHT AS LIBERATION THEOLOGY

The ultimate goal of life is emancipation from discord of every nature and this goal is sure to be attained by all.

— Ernest Holmes

NEW THOUGHT IS EMERGENT

In the 1860s, America found itself in polarizing tensions that threatened to pull the young nation apart. Anti-slavery candidate Abraham Lincoln won the presidency, sparking the birth of the Confederacy. After a bloody Civil War, a new era of reconstruction began, which saw the elevation of African Americans into politics and positions of power and prosperity, only to come crashing down under the subversive dawn of Jim Crow and White backlash, whose aftershocks are still felt today.

The battle for the moral, religious, and scientific ideas that would shape the nation going forward was well underway. The religious landscape had divided itself between a liturgical movement (Catholic, Episcopalian, Lutheran), in which access to God was strictly mediated through the liturgical rights of communal services and ritual engagement, and the evangelical (Baptist) movement, which said God could be experienced through the deeply emotional experience of conversion, while Transcendentalists, like Ralph Waldo Emerson, insisted that God did not need a church at all, as It (God) was as close as the grass under our feet and the in the sway of the trees overhead.

Chart 4.1, "New Thought Is Emergent": New Thought emerges out of the tensions of these three fields as they each battle to define the regulative ideas that will shape the 19th century and beyond.

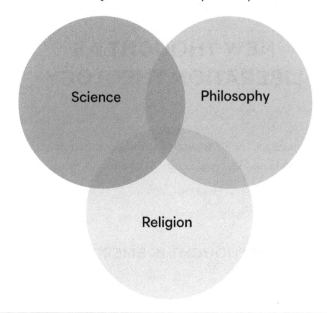

Moreover, it seemed people were being asked to choose between religion and science, which looked to edge God out of the human experience and replace It with the rational logic of empirical results. Meanwhile, the northeast intellectual circles were on the verge of being consumed with explorations of the physic and metaphysical capacities of the mind and consciousness. It is here, in the tensions and polarized positions of these fields (religion, science, and philosophy) that something unique emerged. An eclectic group of thinkers, entrepreneurs, mystics, and charismatic speakers contributed to something that could never seem to be sourced from one among them, yet was proudly claimed by all of them.

The movement that eventually took the name New Thought came into being because there remained a hunger within the intellect, spirit, and soul of the American consciousness to write a new story about who we are and why we are here—a new story deemed necessary because heretofore what religion and science offered proved inadequate.

Something new was emerging. Rather than the fields of science, philosophy, and religion staying neatly in their boxes, these bold pioneer thinkers dared to mash them up—to apply scientific rationalism to questions of God and prayer, and to apply the realm of divinity and the supernatural to material and scientific objectivity. They would dare to replace the angry God of the Old Testament with a Creator whose powers were checked by rational law. They would propose that disease was a physical event, not an expression of divine punishment or retribution. This bold boundary crossing freed intellectual curiosity and pushed the limits toward bold new possibilities that inspired new thoughts.

As John S. Haller explains in the introduction of *The History of New Thought: From Mind Cure to Positive Thinking and the Prosperity Gospel*:

> *Unlike dogma-bound Christians who dwelt on humankind's fall from grace and the need to expiate themselves from sin and darkness, the practitioners who explored these new sciences chose to celebrate life by identifying the spark of divinity in humanity's inner nature. The presumption of humanity's total depravity and of predestination fell before a benevolent Deity operating through known laws, where the intellect alone was free. All that a person was and could be lay within human power that, by inference, was received through an influx of life from the Divine.*

We see then New Thought as an emergent and critical response that arises in three key areas: health (mind-body connection), divinity, and universal wisdom. This pattern of emergence is the first benchmark in seeing New Thought as a Liberation Theology.

EMERGENT RESPONSE TO HEALTH

*The New Thought movement focused its
initial energies on the application of mental
science to health through a combination of the
physical sciences, romantic idealism, Spiritualism, mysticism,
Emersonism, and Swedenborgianism.*

— *John S. Haller,* The History of New Thought

In 1838 in Belfast, Maine, a young and inquisitive clockmaker by the name of Phineas Pankhurst Quimby sat spellbound watching Charles Poyen demonstrate the curious powers unleashed through the emerging science of animal magnetism. This display of physical and physiological phenomena caught the clockmaker's deepest attention, and he sought to learn as much as he could about it, including trying and documenting his own experiments. Animal magnetism and its proponents were the students of Viennese physician Franz Anton Mesmer, the father of what would become known as mesmerism or hypnosis. But over time, Quimby became skeptical whether or not animal magnetism could really be responsible the results he was seeing. Others in the field had begun to speculate that the patients' belief played an important role, but Quimby took it one step further. He proposed that our minds are actually the sum total of our beliefs, and that "if a person is deceived into a belief that he has or is liable to have a disease, the belief is catching and the effects follow from [the belief]."

Thus, what became the Mind-Cure movement arose out of several factors: the primitive state of modern medicine in the 1850s; the quest for alternative solutions and healing, as demonstrated by newspaper advertisements filled with claims of quick cure-alls, health remedies, and miraculous results; and, for Quimby at least, the inadequate solution of Mesmer's method. Quimby claimed that health could be achieved by only overcoming "self-defeating attitudes."

> *All sickness is in the mind or belief. ...*
> *To cure the disease is to correct the error,*
> *destroy the cause, and the effect will cease.*

— *Phineas Parkhurst Quimby,* History of New Thought

By 1861, Quimby opened an office in Boston and documented thousands of healings through his methods. For this he was labeled the "Scientist of Transcendentalism" by Steward Holmes, who wrote, "Quimby demonstrated visibly, on the human organisms, the operational validity of Emerson's hypothesis."

From Quimby to Deepak Chopra, the proponents of the science of positive thinking and the psychological and physiological impact of mind over matter left an indelible impression on the human experience. Modern medicine in Quimby's time lacked solutions for most of the things that ailed us, and Mesmerism relied too heavily on the influence of a mediator, whose own agenda could easily get in the way. Something new had to emerge, putting the power of health and wholeness in the hands (and mind) of those who needed it most.

EMERGENT RESPONSE TO RELATIONSHIP WITH THE DIVINE

Whether due to liturgical or evangelical approaches to our innate desire to be in connection with something bigger than ourselves, many found the religion being preached from the pulpits across America to be old and irrelevant. Many educated Americans, including the likes of Thomas Jefferson and Benjamin Franklin, simply ceased believing that the Christian Bible was any different than other ancient myths. They believed that what was essentially a collection of ancient stories and superstitions required careful scrutinizing based on modern intellectual standards.

According to John S Haller, the lack of faith in the Bible put the era's most progressive thinkers in a precarious spiritual position. They had little to turn to except the intellectually solid but emotionally cold philosophy of Deism.

The 1800s marked a significant period of intellectual and religious change, and Deism emerged as a popular alternative to traditional religious doctrines. Its appeal lay in its rationalistic approach, rejection of religious dogma, and compatibility with scientific advancements. Influential figures, like the Enlightenment philosophers, several of America's Founding Fathers, and literary figures played pivotal roles in spreading Deistic ideas and challenging the authority of established religious institutions. Deism was wildly popular, especially among young people attending college, where intellectual freedom and pushback against "old ideas" was not only trending, but was seen as critically necessary for entering a new era of the burgeoning democracy and "great experiment" called the United States of America. It seemed, for a brief period, that the stronghold of Christianity, its dogmatic beliefs and practices, and its seats of power and authority (held by old White men) would soon be replaced with something new, fresh, intellectually sound, and anchored in reason, albeit still controlled by White men.

While the popularity of Deism waned in the face of 19th century religious revival movements, its impact on shaping religious and intellectual discourse remains significant, highlighting the enduring appeal of reason, skepticism, and a naturalistic understanding of the world, all of which found its way into the DNA of New Thought. Deism was an important precursor to the New Thought movement, though it lacked emotional warmth and reliance on an inward conviction and intuition. One of the primary tenets of Deism was its emphasis on reason and rationality as the basis for understanding the Divine and the world. Deists rejected supernatural revelation and instead relied on the power of human reason to comprehend the natural order of the universe. This commitment to rationality served as a crucial foundation for New Thought, which also sought to reconcile spiritual truths with scientific principles.

New Thought pioneers, such as Quimby and Ralph Waldo Emerson, built on the Deist legacy, emphasizing the power of human intellect and reason in the pursuit of spiritual understanding. Deism introduced the concept of a benevolent and transcendent Creator who set the world in motion but did not actively intervene in human affairs. This belief aligned with the idea of spiritual evolution and progress. Deists viewed humanity as capable of moral improvement and saw history as a progression toward enlightenment and social harmony.

This notion of spiritual evolution resonated with New Thought's early thinkers, who posited that individuals had the power to grow spiritually and consciously align themselves with higher spiritual laws. New Thought teachings emphasized personal development, self-improvement, and the realization of each person's divine potential. Deism challenged traditional religious divisions and emphasized the unity of all humanity under a common Creator. It rejected religious exclusivity and encouraged a more inclusive and universal approach to spirituality. Similarly, New Thought stressed the interconnectedness of all individuals and the inherent unity of humanity. It promoted the idea that all individuals were interconnected through a shared Divine essence and that recognizing this unity could lead to harmony, peace, and spiritual growth. Both Deism and New Thought advocated for a broader understanding of spirituality that transcended religious boundaries and fostered a sense of interconnectedness. Once again, emerging out of the inadequate theological constructs of mainline religion, New Thought emerged to push the boundaries, imaginations, and spiritual experiences of its followers.

EMERGENT RESPONSE TO TRUTH

The final way in which New Thought is emergent has propelled the movement into the broad space of interfaith and secular humanism with equal conviction. While most religious movements seek to define their borders of thought, beliefs, and practices, New Thought takes a very different approach. The early New Thought writers, largely influenced by Emerson, believed they were tapping into something that was universal in nature and, as such, evidence for the "truth" of New Thought could be seen and discovered throughout various traditions and philosophies around the world.

In other words, New Thought committed to being an open system, and what it claimed for its "truths and principles" in fact did not belong exclusively to New Thought but to the Universe itself, free to be claimed by anyone during their own discovery process. As such, the dogmatic, close-minded, and exclusive nature that most religions took to their beliefs was a direct cause for New Thought thinkers to go their own way. Despite the fact that many of them considered themselves progressive Christians, they could not imagine themselves as reformers from within the traditions they came from. New Thought's approach to understanding God was, therefore, anchored in a commitment to intellectual freedom.

Ironically, this defining hallmark of the movement was solidified in the late 1890s when Mary Baker Eddy, founder of Christian Science (the earliest and fastest growing expression of New Thought at the time), began excommunicating women whom she had previously entrusted for diverging from her own words. In Eddy's mind, she had been given the inspiration of Christian Science straight from God, with no help from anyone, despite being a student healed by Quimby's methods. After several such purging waves of independent thinkers around her, she went so far as to say that if others outside of her control were going to call the movement "New Thought," then she wanted it made clear that the term did not include her and her Christian Science movement. Others were false teachings, and she had the truth.

Yet the commitment to intellectual freedom and diverse interpretations of New Thought persisted. The movement grew rapidly, with many expressions and teachings spread through magazines, pamphlets, churches, and the like. By the time the World's Fair came to Chicago in 1896, New Thought was a well-established presence, thanks to the popularity of Eddy's most successful rejected student, Emma Curtis Hopkins. Both Hopkins and Eddy were at the Word's Fair, but they were not on speaking terms. Hopkins was in the Women's Pavilion and Eddy in the World Religions Pavilion. By 1895, Emma Curtis Hopkins had moved to Chicago, opened a School of Divinity, and was teaching hundreds of students, primarily women. These students spread out throughout the nation and opened their own branches, started magazines, and taught classes expressing their own interpretation of New Thought wisdom from coast to coast.

NEW THOUGHT IS CONTEXTUAL

As discussed in Chapter Three, the second principle of liberation theologies is that they are traditionally contextualized answers to a particular need and to a particular group of people: the need, for example, for poor people to know that God is on their side (Catholic liberation theology) or, in the case of Black liberation theology, the belief that African Americans can have faith that God not only knows their pain and struggle, but that God does not stand outside of their struggle (i.e., God is Black).

Here we don't see evidence of New Thought being a contextualized response in the same way as other forms of liberation theology. But context can be framed in two distinct directions. Context can be particular (Latin, Black, LGBTQIA+, etc.), or context can be universal (human). It is the latter we see in New Thought—the desire to create a universal context inclusive of all humanity who would have the ears to hear.

One might believe that New Thought is originally contextualized by White men of economic and social status (privilege) who had the time and resources to engage in the intellectual musings of high society. Such was certainly the case for the Transcendental Club of Boston. However, while there is no doubt that a White male normative haze hangs over the movement to this day, something we'll address in Chapter Six on reconciliation, to characterize New Thought in its entirety by this Achilles' heel would be to miss the diverse ways in which the teaching was adopted, contextualized, popularized, and contributed to by those outside the dominant class in its earliest days.

Together, the expressions outlined below give way to something unique among liberation theologies. First, there is an insistence that the practice can be contextualized by anyone because the principles are universal. And second, the practice can have a practical contextualization by women, people of color, and those who live outside North America. These two threads remain direct links to New Thought's liberation history, as we will explore in the next chapter.

CONTEXTUALIZED BY WOMEN

New Thought as the popular ideology of the 20th century consumer capitalism does not take into account the first thirty years of the movement (1875-1905). ... New Thought followers understood themselves to be part of a women's movement that would herald a new "women's era."

— *Beryl Satter,* Each Mind a Kingdom

In her book, *Each Mind a Kingdom: American Women, Sexual Purity, and the New Thought Movement, 1875-1920*, Beryl Satter makes the case, compellingly so, that women have not only been at the forefront of the New Thought movement but that they also shaped the language and expression of principles based on their understanding of gender norms barriers and mental constructs.

At a time when women faced numerous societal restrictions, the New Thought movement provided a platform for them to express their ideas, contribute to spiritual discourse, and advocate for gender equality. Satter's work explores the significant role of women in the New Thought movement, highlighting their leadership, writings, and efforts to challenge gender norms and promote spiritual empowerment for all.

Women played crucial roles as leaders and spiritual guides within the New Thought movement. Figures such as Emma Curtis Hopkins, Myrtle Fillmore, and H. Emilie Cady emerged as influential voices, establishing their own churches, opening teaching centers, and publishing works that shaped the movement's principles and practices. These women challenged traditional gender roles and demonstrated their capacity for spiritual leadership, inspiring others to embrace their own divine potential and become active participants in their spiritual journeys.

Women's contributions to the New Thought movement extended through their writings and publications. Myrtle Fillmore, cofounder of Unity, wrote *Healing Letters* and *How to Let God Help You,* which became foundational texts within the movement. Other women, like Elizabeth Towne and Nona L. Brooks, established publishing houses and produced magazines and books that disseminated New Thought ideas. Through their writings, women brought forth perspectives on personal empowerment, healing, and the transformative power of the mind, leaving a lasting impact on the movement's literature.

New Thought provided a platform for women to advocate for social reform and challenge gender inequality. Women within the movement promoted equality, emphasizing that spiritual power and potential were not gender exclusive. Many New Thought organizations embraced progressive ideas, such as women's suffrage, education, and economic independence. Women in the movement worked to dismantle traditional gender roles and empower individuals, regardless of gender, to recognize their inherent worth and live fulfilling lives.

CONTEXTUALIZED IN JAPAN

In Japan, there is a syncretic, monotheistic, New Thought Japanese religion that has spread since the end of World War II. It emphasizes gratitude for nature, the family, ancestors, and, above all, religious faith in one universal God. Seichō No Ie, "The Home of Infinite Life, Wisdom, and Abundance," is the world's largest New Thought organization. By the end of 2010, it had more than 1.6 million followers and 442 facilities, mostly located in Japan. Seichō No Ie began with the writings of its founder, Masaharu Taniguchi, in 1930.

Both Ernest and Fenwicke Holmes took interest in the Japanese style of New Thought and contributed to the movement's growth. In particular, Fenwicke helped co-author *The Science of Faith,* which became a cornerstone text in the growth of the movement.

CONTEXTUALIZED BY AFRICAN AMERICANS

New Thought as led, developed, and expressed by African Americans has a rich history firmly rooted in a liberation theology framework. African American leaders within the New Thought movement faced unique challenges due to racial discrimination and segregation. Despite these obstacles, they made significant contributions to the movement's growth and development.

They emphasized the importance of self-determination, racial pride, and spiritual empowerment. African American leaders within New Thought also advocated for social justice, challenging systemic racism and promoting inclusivity and equality within spiritual communities.

"Father Divine," an early architect of street or social gospel and justice work woven into ministry, credits the teachings of New Thought and the work of Charles Fillmore and Mary Baker Eddy for inspiring his ministry.

The Universal Foundation for Better Living (UFBL) stands as a significant African American-led organization within the New Thought movement. Founded by Reverend Johnnie Colemon in the mid-20th century, UFBL focused on spiritual teachings that embraced African American culture, community, and social justice. The organization emphasized personal empowerment, self-love, and the recognition of the divine spark within every individual. UFBL continues to foster spiritual growth and empowerment within African American communities in the United States, Jamaica and Canada.

We cannot speak of the influence, impact, and contribution of African Americans in New Thought without the indomitable Rev. Ike (Frederick J. Eikerenkoetter II). Rev. Ike was a pioneering force who crossed boundaries. In true New Thought's universal teaching form, he belonged to no one but commanded great respect in the evangelical movement, in Black churches, and in New Thought circles alike. And in true "New Thought is heretical" fashion, he drew great criticism as well. Yet his reach was undeniable and his impact without peer. In long overdue recognition his life and ministry, Rev. Ike now is memorialized in the Smithsonian's exhibit on Black life in America and in a new book entitled *Rev. Ike: An Extraordinary Life of Influence,* co-authored by his son, Xavier Eikerenkoetter, and Mark Victor Hansen. Rev. Ike filled the radio airwaves, TV broadcasts, and stadiums like Madison Square Garden with African American followers who learned to shake off the "old pie in the sky, sweet by-and-by visions of heavenly blessings" in favor of affirming, claiming, and believing in our divine right to prosperity and goodness now.

We would be remiss also not to highlight the profound work of Bishop Dr. Barbara King in Atlanta. In the 1970s, Dr. Barbara King built the "Church on the Hill" in Southside Atlanta. She faced many battles as an African American women and senior pastor. Whether it was because she was called to build her church in the "poor side of town" or because she was a women faith leader (rare and frowned upon in the Black church), or just because she was Black, her detractors were many, and she proved them all wrong in spectacular fashion. Today, if you fly into Atlanta through Hartsfield-Jackson International Airport (the busiest airport in the world), you might walk past the Bishop Dr. Barbara King International Prayer Chapel. To say she left her mark and legacy on the city of Atlanta is an understatement.

And from the Religious Science/Centers for Spiritual Living tradition we have Rev. Dr. Michael Bernard Beckwith, who rose from the tutelage of Dr. Dan Morgan of Guidance Church to found the Agape International Truth Center in Los Angeles. Dr. Beckwith went on to build an international ministry that draws the attention of Oprah Winfrey, Stevie Wonder, Van Morison, Madonna, and many other artists and creatives in Hollywood and beyond.

Each of these ministers embodied the ethos of self-empowerment and relied on the "God within" to give life to profoundly important works that each continue to resonate and contribute to the movement as a whole.

NEW THOUGHT LIBERATION
AS THE BYPRODUCT OF THE
APPLICATION OF NEW THOUGHT

The third principle of liberation theologies is that they are byproducts of living out the implications of the primary theology, previously referred to as living out the radical implications of the teaching. The New Thought movement promotes the principles of oneness, inclusion, harmony, and a kind of spiritual equality (that the laws of the universe are equally and instantly available to all). These ideas, when lived by adherents, will inevitably lead followers to believe and act on behalf of the empowerment of all people. The principles lead directly away from exclusion and power dynamics that keep humanity in oppressive dynamics and structures.

While much of its 150-year history focused on this work of personal empowerment and spiritual awakening, modern day New Thought expands into areas of collective awakening and social concerns. In reality, this work always comprised part of the movement, but it received less attention during much of New Thought's history. Today, it is more common than in the recent past to hear how the philosophy and principles of New Thought positively impact issues of social justice and collective consciousness. Adherents of New Thought are beginning to realize that the world that works for everyone they envision will only be made manifest through the hands of those willing to build it.

Put simply, you cannot continue to practice the principles of New Thought while remaining ignorant of or indifferent to the ways in which consciousness creates inequity just as much as it creates liberation. Chapter Six, Reconciliation, offers a more robust discussion of these concepts.

EXPLORING THE CHARACTERISTICS
OF A LIBERATION THEOLOGY
FROM A NEW THOUGHT LENS

In Chapter Three, we defined the characteristics of liberation theology as the following: solidarity with the oppressed, affirmation of our inherent state of being, unifying with a liberating force or power, and being political in nature and religious in commitment.

SOLIDARITY WITH THE OPPRESSED OR MARGINALIZED

At first blush, it may seem that New Thought/Science of Mind does not meet the standard of solidarity with the oppressed or marginalized. We do not have a theological praxis for economic justice, ministry to the poor, or direct social action for the uplift of the marginalized in our society. So it seems right from the start that New Thought and Science of Mind do not qualify as a liberation theology. In fact, this was my position when I first encountered liberation theology in college. I thought, "These are beautiful theological approaches, but Science of Mind doesn't have this same perspective or approach." But if it were that easy to dismiss, I would not have written this book.

Let's take a closer look at how traditional liberation theology approaches the task of solidarity with the oppressed and marginalized.

Liberation theology makes the case that despite world conditions, social norms, or collective consciousness about or of a particular group or class of people, they are, in fact, one with God—divine, blessed, and the sacred property of the Almighty. The act of solidarity is made by lifting the identified class of people into equal status, if not specialized or divine status in the eyes of God.

In this light, what is among the most common phrase heard when first attending a New Thought or Science of Mind center? The affirmation: "I am one with God," or "I am one with Love/Wholeness," or something similar. In other words, one of the first distinguishing acts of a New Thought community is to lift each person into a state of identifying as one with the Divine, regardless of class, status, race, or station in life. As such, anyone who at any time may identify or be identified by society as marginalized will find that the first task in a New Thought community is to claim your oneness with that Power and Presence that transcends marginalized status.

AFFIRMING OUR NATURAL STATE

Building on the first characteristic of liberation theology, the second characteristic is the affirmation of the identified group's natural state.

Liberation theology asserts that oppression, poverty, and other forms of marginalization are not natural or God-ordained states. The condition and the constructs that support it, that is the sin—not those who are subjected to it.

Likewise in New Thought, conditions are just that, conditions. Temporary and the manifestation of error thinking, they are not our natural state. Our natural state is wholeness, divinity, perfection, prosperity, and love. What New Thought calls "error thinking" produces so-called negative conditions. Error thinking occurs both in the individual's immediate subjective state of consciousness and in institutionalized systems and structures in society that perpetuate, reinforce, and indeed are built on such error thinking.

However, the pure essence of who we are is the quality and nature of God, since God is all that there is. Therefore, our natural state of being is in the harmony and wholeness of God. This idea is harkens back to the work of Quimby, who rested his healing practice on the idea that there is a wholeness within each person as their true nature and that alignment with that mentally brings forth experience of that physically.

Ernest Holmes, founder of Religious Science and Science of Mind, said, "There is a power in the universe greater than you are, and you can use it." This captures the emphasis New Thought, in all its expressions, places on uniting followers with a "power within" that can free, liberate, or emancipate them from mental blocks and hidden beliefs in limitation, lack, and unworthiness. Other ways in which this expresses itself in the lexicon of New Thought is through phrases such as, "Change your thinking, change your life," "Thoughts become things," and so on.

LIBERATION THEOLOGY IS POLITICAL IN NATURE AND RELIGIOUS IN COMMITMENT

What does it mean to be political in nature but religious in commitment?

Many think that to be political these days is to be confrontational, divisive, polarizing—all things most clergy would want to avoid, or at least the ones without a self-defined prophetic or moral mandate. And, of course, the vast number of people filling the pews of spiritual communities have the same desire not to not cause trouble or be wrapped up in divisive positions and conversations with their friends, coworkers, and fellow sojourners in spiritual community.

But as Gandhi said, "Those who believe there is no politics in religion do not understand either." So, what does it really mean to be political?

In simple terms, being political means to engage in politics. Politics is defined as the ways and means by which groups of people make decisions that govern the collective lives of a people (group, tribe, etc). These days, it seams everything is political. Well, that's because everything is. Virtually every aspect of our social lives warrants discussion at some level that will be political in nature. As established in the beginning of this book, our lives are governed by story—the story we tell ourselves and each other. Religion is a major carrier of those stories, and the other major carrier is our political discourse. Political friction and discourse in a society are merely the struggle over which story we are going to tell and how we are going to tell it. All stories, whether they are political or religious, are consciousness expressing.

This has always been the case, yet somehow middle-class, Protestant, White America has bought into the illusion that there is a magical divide between what is political and what is not—and that the political stuff can be quarantined out of our daily affairs and segregated out of our churches. This illusion, more than the topics themselves, is what is causing harm.

But just because the reality is that most of our social life involves topics that touch politics or governance in some way does not mean that politics has to carry with it the heavy and toxic energy that often accompanies the term. When we say that someone is being "too political" or that a topic is "too political" and therefore ought to be avoided in polite company—be that a church, online, or elsewhere—what we are saying is that the topic has become politicized. It has become a political football or wedge, tossed to and fro between politicians as a means to agitate the general public into taking a position either for or against a given topic. Once this occurs, the topic magically becomes a political (aka, divisive) topic.

Sadly, what the politicians know is that once this happens, a critical mass of us will choose to avoid the topic altogether, leaving the space wide open for politicians to decide their own course of action, absent input from their constituents, or of only their supporting constituents. In other words, part of politicians' story is that we will be turned off by political culture war topics, which is exactly what they need us to be so they can do with the topic what they will.

One of my high school teachers had a sign in her classroom that read: "Not to decide is to decide." Politics in church or spiritual communities operate by the same principle—to not engage is to engage. Too many well-meaning spiritual folks hold it as an admirable value of their spiritual practice to avoid "political" topics, yet they are not avoiding them at all. Instead, they are playing the disengaged role that politicians hope they will.

Breaking the fever of allergic reactionism here takes two things. First is the wake-up call that politics (the story of how we govern life) touches everything, far more topics that we'd like it to, and that is not going to change. Second is the realization that while politics touches everything, that does not mean that everything has to be politicized (put into divisive context), that, indeed, there are topics that don't belong in the mouths of politicians. The topics of culture wars need to be reclaimed by the spiritual and ethical voices of our society and thereby remain on the alter of humanity. That's the role of the prophetic voice —to reclaim and snatch from the jaws of political cannibalism the topics that belong on the altar of human dignity.

In 1956, Ernest Holmes discovered that someone took it upon themselves to alter the alphabetical listings of churches in his Science of Mind magazine, moving the Eastside Church of Los Angeles from first to last, and adding an asterisk that read *"colored church"* at the bottom of the page. Holmes wasted no time in reaching out and calling the minister of that church, Rev. J. Arthur Twyne, to apologize. He also offered to speak at the church the following Sunday, which he did. To the congregation he said, as recounted in *The Essential Ernest Holmes,* "I have been told that too many non-Caucasians attend these lectures. True, there are Caucasians and non-Caucasians in this congregation. But this we must affirm: We are all children of One Living God—One Life that permeates all, without exception—One Intelligence that governs all—and, most important, every man and woman who abides in the universe is a significant entity in the One Universal Consciousness. Our doors will forever be open to all. Whoever you are, be proud—you are a Divine Idea in the Mind of God."

His actions were political in nature because they dealt head on with the social tensions of the era, and they were religious in commitment in that his ultimate goal was to embody the oneness he believed the movement stood for.

Similarly, when Rev. Raymond Charles Barker was greeted by the manager of the New York hotel where his congregation met, he was asked if the colored people attending wouldn't mind using the side entrance for servants, as they were apparently making hotel guests uncomfortable. Dr. Barker removed his congregation from that hotel and never stepped foot in it again. His actions were political in nature and religious in commitment.

Examining New Thought through the lens of the principles and characteristics of liberation theology makes a compelling case for considering New Thought itself to be a liberation theology. A great part of the reason why the case is strong is because it's not new. In New Thought, we often describe our movement as "New Thought, Ancient Wisdom," referring to the not-so-new ideas within New Thought that have deeper roots than the history of the movement itself.

In similar fashion, the history of liberation theology within New Thought is not new either. It, too, extends back with roots deeper than the historical development of liberation theology itself. ∞

REFLECTION QUESTIONS

1. In what ways is New Thought a reflection of liberation theology? Does the author make a compelling case for this premise?

2. How does New Thought framed in liberation theology change the direction of the story New Thought offers?

3. What role do "political" topics play in your experience of New Thought spirituality? Do you think they have a place in the pulpit to be discussed or should they be avoided all together? Where and how do you draw a line?

_____

_____

_____

_____

_____

_____

_____

_____

_____

_____

_____

_____

_____

_____

CHAPTER 5

RADICAL ROOTS

*When the [collective] finally understands and is
conscious of the Oneness of All–then will Separateness and Self-
ishness drop away like a cast-off cloak, and that which we call sin
and injustice can no longer exist.*

— William Walker Atkinson, The Law of the New Thought

Throughout the history of the New Thought movement, a multitude of influences, streams of thought, and philosophy mixed together freely and without reservation. New Thought can hardly lay claim to being a fixed system of beliefs, especially in its early days. Individuals with divergent views have and will always equally find comfort and a home within New Thought.

The movement's history and relationship with social change and justice is no exception. Some will say that the focus on external conditions is beneath our primary task of establishing right order within each person's individual consciousness. Others, on the other hand, would claim that the demonstration of our oneness is proof that we actually believe it. To some degree, both would be right. This conversation is not new. The debate between inner and outer work has taken place since the early days, and it's reaching a new climatic chapter now. This conversation and, as a result, this part of our story continues to evolve.

One common refrain of resistance to New Thought taking on the work, message, or tone of social justice under its wing is the idea that

New Thought has *always* been about the individual. "We teach people how to think, not what to think." I've been reminded of this dozens of times and often with a physical index finger wave to help get the point across. The principle at hand is sound and does not waiver under the light of social justice examination. Indeed, if consciousness is everything and we teach how consciousness works, and if political structures, laws, and ideals are merely forms of consciousness imposing their effect on our collective experience, then knowing how consciousness works (by understanding how to think) is critically important to the process of both individual and societal change.

Nevertheless, what critics of social justice praxis in New Thought are getting at when they use this form of critique is that we are in the business of "minding our own business" with a sole and devoted focus on our internal thought processes. The silent implication here is that focus on external conditions (such as our collective social state) is not only undesirable, it also is bad form or an improper use of the tools of consciousness. Thus, what we really see happening when people defend the position that New Thought ought not be engaged in political issues of any kind is a form of shaming and deflection, rather than a skilled application of the teaching. In relationship to the principle of oneness on which our teaching is based, it's spiritual gaslighting.

These critics further bolster their case by claiming "its always been this way," and for them, that's probably true. But on the whole, this is not the case. Too often, we make the mistake of confusing our limited experience with the universal truth of something, ignorant of the history that precedes us, even as we act as history's fiercest defenders. In reality, what we are actually defending is our own comfortable understanding of the truth or the way it has always been for us.

New Thought as the religion of self-responsibility, success, and prosperity is, surprisingly, a recent turn in our relatively short history. More importantly, this recent turn of focus tracks with the capitalist success and development of American culture and society. In *Each Mind a Kingdom: American Women, Sexual Purity, and the New Thought Movement, 1875-1920,* author Beryl Setter explores the early themes of New Thought teachings through its heavily female-based leadership. These early movement builders were simultaneously intertwined with the women's suffrage movement. This predominately White and upper-class group of women were editors and well-known contributors and distributors of various monthly pamphlets, like *The Dial* and a dozen others, whose content was a mix of New Thought philosophy and social empowerment commentary that fed the suffrage movement. It is safe to say that we cannot effectively appreciate or understand New Thought history without a study of the women's suffrage movement and vice versa. They went hand in hand and, therefore, so too did New Thought principles and the social justice causes of the day.

That is until, as Setter explicitly points to, the turn in the movement and its association to the gender of its leadership:

> *By the early twentieth century, the social and cultural context within which New Thought had flourished began to change. Technological and managerial innovations definitively pushed the United States from an industrial producer to a corporate consumer economy ... and New Thought, the religion of the women's era, would transform into an almost unrecognizable religion of success for the corporate era.*

Certainly, we cannot ignore that our teaching effectively emerged out of the quest for individual healing. However, New Thought history is not a single track progressing from the mind cure movement of the late 1800s. In true American fashion, New Thought is an amalgamation of various streams of consciousness that converged in the late 1800s to give birth to something unique in the religious landscape.

Furthermore, New Thought actually is not new. It is ancient wisdom—and goes much deeper than the last 150 years. Ancient wisdom is rooted in Brown and Black peoples' histories, spirituality, and liberation quest to know themselves and the world around them. Throughout New Thought, not enough credit is given to the ancient cultures that had a relationship to Spirit and higher consciousness that was direct, intuition based, and directed by consciousness. And while Ernest Holmes gave credit to the Greek philosophers and the Filmores of Unity for the ways in which they were inspired by Egyptian culture, this recognition still does not get enough attention in today's examination of the roots of New Thought. First Nation Peoples' relationship to Spirit has always been an intimate, vision-led, and intuition-guided spirituality, rooted in their understanding of the oneness of the universe. Similarly, the mysticism embedded in African spirituality, such as VooDoo, Yorba, Akan, just to name a few, far predates the promotion of intuitive and contemplative practices in the West.

To understand what the New Thought movement is beyond its recent history, we must understand the contextual backdrop that gave rise to it in America in the late 1800s. Most depictions of New Thought history begin the story with a clockmaker from New England, Phineas Parkhurst Quimby, and so the legacy goes on in a seemingly straight line from Quimby to Mary Baker Eddy to Emma Curtis Hopkins to the Filmores and Holmes. But New Thought History has more branches on the tree.

New Thought was birthed from the convergence of three major movements in American spiritual and religious history—Mind Cure Movement, the Transcendentalist Movement, and Progressive Liberal Christianity—one of which is heavily overlooked in most New Thought communities.

We discussed in the previous chapter the Mind Cure Movement and Quimby, the lasting gifts of which are the mind-body connection, the equality in access to the power of the Mind, and the understanding that innate wholeness and harmony are the fundamental order of the universe. Now let's look at the other contributing movements to New Thought.

TRANSCENDENTALISM

In 1836, a group of rebellious Unitarian preachers gathered in the home of George Ripley of Boston. They called themselves "The Transcendental Club," which included some of the era's greatest thinkers: Ralph Waldo Emerson, Theodore Parker, William H. Channing, James Freeman Clarke, and others. Soon they would be joined by the likes of Henry David Thoreau, Margaret Fuller, Elizabeth Peabody, and Branson Alcott. The women of this group would go on to contribute to and oversee numerous publications, amassing thousands of readers across the nation. In these publications, they shared their New Thought ideas. Together, this group held a common rejection of the cold intellectualism that dominated the broadly embraced religions of their day. And while they were far too independent-minded for conformity, they were able to agree to three basic principles:

1. The immanence of God
2. Inward experience as primary authority
3. A rejection of all external authority

In his book *American Metaphysical Religion*, Ronnie Pontiac writes, "This new vision of the self's inner-connection with God rendered biblical notions of sin and vicarious atonement obsolete. In the transcendentalist view, what separated us from God is not disobedience but rather limited self-awareness."

Ralph Waldo Emerson, renowned American philosopher, poet, and essayist, held strong abolitionist beliefs during a time when slavery was deeply entrenched in America. Through his writings, speeches, and activism, Emerson passionately advocated for the abolition of slavery and the inherent equality of all individuals.

Emerson based his abolitionist stance on several key factors. First and foremost was his deep commitment to individual freedom and human dignity. As a transcendentalist, Emerson believed in the inherent worth and divinity of every human being, irrespective of race or social status. He saw slavery as a grave injustice that violated the fundamental principles of liberty and equality, and he sought to expose and confront this moral and social evil.

Another influence on Emerson was his exposure to the realities of slavery through his interactions with abolitionist circles and from first-hand accounts. He had close relationships with prominent abolitionists, including William Lloyd Garrison and Frederick Douglass, who shared their experiences and insights with him. These encounters and the vivid descriptions of the horrors of slavery fueled Emerson's conviction to speak out against it.

Further solidifying Emerson's abolitionist stance was his belief in the power of moral reform and social progress. He believed individuals had the capacity to transform society through their actions and ideas. Emerson saw the abolitionist cause as an opportunity to ignite change and create a more just and humane society. He saw the fight against slavery as a moral imperative, and his writings and speeches served as a call to action for others to join the cause.

In his influential essay "The American Scholar," Emerson emphasized the importance of intellectual and moral independence. He argued that individuals should question societal norms and institutions and act in accordance with their consciences. This call for individual autonomy and critical thinking aligned with his abolitionist beliefs, as he urged individuals to question and reject the unjust institution of slavery.

Emerson's abolitionist stance was not limited to his writings and philosophical musings; he actively engaged in public activism. He delivered numerous lectures denouncing slavery and attended anti-slavery conventions. Emerson also financially supported anti-slavery causes and used his platform to raise awareness and rally support for the abolitionist movement.

Theodore Parker was a transcendentalist and one of Boston's leading social reformers. He began his career as a Unitarian minister, but his radical theological views caused many of his Unitarian ministerial colleagues to ostracize him by refusing to exchange pulpits with him. In 1845, he left the Unitarian Church of West Roxbury to become minister of Boston's independent 28th Congregational Society of Boston. His congregation grew rapidly, with as many as three thousand people gathered for a Sunday worship service. That number represented almost 2 percent of the population of Boston at the time. Some of those who attended were among the most prominent anti-slavery and social justice activists of their time, including Senator Charles Sumner, educator Horace Mann, and abolitionist William Lloyd Garrison.

Parker called repeatedly for noncompliance with the Fugitive Slave Law. In a sermon immediately after passage of the law (November 1850), he said, "It is the natural duty of citizens to rescue every fugitive slave from the hands of the marshal who essays to return him to bondage; to do it peaceably if they can, forcibly if they must, but by all means to do it."

These words demonstrate Parker's commitment to living out a faith that was political in nature and religious in commitment.

The Transcendental Movement, which emerged in the early 19th century in the United States, had a profound impact on the New Thought movement and its guiding principles. Rooted in the belief in the inherent goodness of individuals and their connection to nature and the Divine, transcendentalists sought to foster personal and societal transformation. Transcendentalism encompassed several key tenets that went on to greatly influence the New Thought movement:

Individualism: Transcendentalists emphasized the importance of individual autonomy, and the pursuit of personal truth. They believed every person possesses inherent wisdom and has the capacity to access divine knowledge within themselves. Though we should note this emphasis on the individual is often mischaracterized as being free of social responsibility or relations, this is not what the transcendentalists sought to emphasize. Rather, they focused on the belief that an awakening of one's empowered self would lead to greater connection and service to the collective good of all.

Nature's Divinity: Transcendentalists saw nature as a source of spiritual inspiration and believed in its inherent divinity. They advocated for a harmonious relationship with the natural world, recognizing that the well-being of humanity was intertwined with the preservation of the environment.

Intuition and Imagination: Transcendentalists valued intuition and imagination as pathways to higher truth and spiritual enlightenment. They encouraged individuals to trust their inner voices, cultivating a deeper understanding of themselves and their connections to the world.

The Transcendental Movement played a significant role in shaping the social justice movement, particularly in the areas of abolitionism, women's rights, and environmental activism.

Abolitionism: Transcendentalists, deeply influenced by their belief in the inherent worth and equality of all individuals, actively supported the abolitionist cause. They condemned slavery as a violation of human dignity and championed the emancipation of enslaved people. Transcendentalists such as Emerson, Thoreau, and Theodore Parker delivered powerful speeches and writings denouncing slavery, calling for its immediate abolition and inspiring future generations of activists.

Women's Rights: The Transcendental Movement also contributed to the advancement of women's rights. Margaret Fuller, a prominent transcendentalist, played a crucial role in advocating for women's equality and education. Her writings, including *Woman in the Nineteenth Century,* challenged societal norms and called for women's intellectual and social liberation. The Transcendental Movement's emphasis on individualism and the inherent worth of every person helped pave the way for the women's suffrage movement and the broader fight for gender equality.

Environmental Activism: The transcendentalists' reverence for nature and their belief in the interconnectedness of all living beings laid the foundation for modern environmental activism. Thoreau's masterpiece, *On Walden Pond,* encouraged a profound appreciation for nature and the need to preserve it. This work, along with the writings of other transcendentalists, inspired later environmentalists to advocate for conservation, sustainable living, and ecological justice. The Transcendental Movement's spiritual connection to nature had a lasting impact on the environmental movement, reminding us of our responsibility to protect the Earth for future generations.

The principles of the Transcendental Movement continue to resonate in contemporary social justice movements. The emphasis on individual autonomy, personal truth, and the interconnectedness of all beings serves as a rallying cry for equality, human rights, and environmental stewardship.

The concept of interconnectedness promotes the recognition that all forms of oppression are intertwined and must be addressed collectively. Movements for racial justice, LGBTQIA+ rights, and economic equality draw inspiration from this interconnected view, recognizing that the liberation of one group is inseparable from the liberation of all.

The belief in personal truth and the power of individual agency inspires activists to challenge societal norms, question unjust systems, and advocate for transformative change. The Transcendental Movement's call for self-reflection and the cultivation of inner wisdom continues to guide activists seeking social justice, encouraging them to trust their instincts, amplify marginalized voices, and imagine a more just and equitable society.

PROGRESSIVE LIBERAL THEOLOGY

New Thought is heavily influenced by the long stream of progressive liberal theology, by those who dared to push the boundaries of ridged dogmatic structures and to ask all of Christendom to think differently—a collection of reformers who, through their "new thoughts," challenged the dominant structures and principalities, from Orgen of Alexandria to Ralph Waldo Emerson, Paul Tillich, and John Shelby Spong to Bishop Dr. Yvette Flunder, D.E. Paulk, and Carlton Pearson. Beginning in the earliest days, the first several centuries of organized Christianity, allegorical interpretation of scripture was more popular than any form of literal translation. In other words, they knew then that scriptures were primarily teaching tools that used symbols and metaphor more than eyewitness accounts to actual events.

Progressive Liberal Christianity is a dynamic movement and practice that emphasizes open-mindedness, inclusivity, and a commitment to social justice. It seeks to reconcile traditional Christian teachings with contemporary social realities, engaging in critical dialogue with other disciplines and perspectives. Based on a set of principles, Progressive Liberal Christianity has a profound relationship with social justice, illustrating how this approach to faith provides a platform for compassionate action and transformative change in the world. Moreover, this theology is far less interested in literal translations of scripture or dogmatic traditions than it is with embodying a Christ ethic of "love your neighbor" and "they shall know you by your fruits." These values put them closer on the spectrum to New Thought than not.

In fact, most, if not all, of the early New Thought movement organizers considered themselves and their body of work Christian (in the most liberal/progressive sense). The New Thought lineage (Emerson, Quimby, Eddy, Hopkins, Fillmore, Holmes) is full of those who sought to redefine Christianity in a manner that reclaimed and restored (in their minds) the original intent of being:

1. A follower of the way (not the man)—as did the early first century Christians, and as they were called;

2. Understanding the healing power of conscious contact with the Divine; and

3. Holders of an allegorical and mystical truth that transcended cultures and dogma (even as it was turned into one).

Thus, their efforts were to reach back to those basic ideas and practices, even if they were rejected by the mainline groups. As such, it was not so much about reforming the institutions (as the institutions expressed no interest in the works of New Thought authors), but rather preserving and re-presenting the ancient truth and practices. In practicality, they considered themselves more Christian than most of those who used the label. At the same time the movement today often seeks a post-Christian position, even while its roots are deeply embedded within the larger progressive Christian context.

The gap between Christianity and New Thought has been closing rapidly over the last one hundred years—from the radically inclusive coalition building of the Fellowship of Affirming Ministries and the wide-open tent of the United Church of Christ today to the dogma-breaking sermons of Baptist preacher Rev. Henry Emerson Fosdick of the 1930s.

Here is an excerpt of Fosdick's 1922 most famous sermon, entitled "Shall the Fundamentalist Win?":

> *As I plead thus for an intellectually hospitable, tolerant, liberty-loving church, I am of course thinking primarily about this new generation. We have boys and girls growing up in our homes and schools, and because we love them, we may well wonder about the church that will be waiting to receive them. Now the worst kind of church that can possibly be offered to the allegiance of the new generation is an intolerant church. Ministers often bewail the fact that young people turn from religion to science for the regulative ideas of their lives. But this is easily explicable. Science treats a young man's mind as though it were really important. A scientist says to a young man: "Here is the universe challenging our investigation. Here are the truths we have seen, so far. Come, study with us! See what we already have seen and then look further to see more, for science is an intellectual adventure for the truth." Can you imagine any man who is worthwhile turning from that call to the church if the church seems to him to say, "Come, and we will feed you opinions from a spoon. No thinking is allowed*

here except such as brings you to certain specified, predetermined con-clusions. These prescribed opinions we will give you in advance of your thinking; now think, but only so as to reach these results."

PRINCIPLES OF PROGRESSIVE LIBERAL CHRISTIANITY

Openness to New Interpretations: Progressive Liberal Christianity embraces diverse interpretations of scripture and recognizes the evolving nature of human understanding. It encourages critical engagement with the Bible and an openness to new insights, recognizing that religious truths can be found in a variety of sources.

Inclusive Love and Acceptance: Progressive Liberal Christianity emphasizes the unconditional love and acceptance of all individuals, regardless of their race, gender, sexual orientation, or socioeconomic background. It rejects discrimination and seeks to create inclusive communities that celebrate diversity.

Social Justice and Human Rights: Deeply rooted in the pursuit of social justice and human rights, Progressive Liberal Christianity acknowledges that faith calls for actively addressing systemic injustices, such as poverty, racism, sexism, and environmental degradation. It advocates for the equitable distribution of resources, the dismantling of oppressive structures, and the empowerment of marginalized communities.

Interfaith Dialogue and Cooperation: Progressive Liberal Christianity promotes interfaith dialogue and cooperation, recognizing the value of engaging with other religious traditions and perspectives. It seeks common ground and collaboration in addressing shared social challenges and working toward a more peaceful and just world.

Engaging with Science and Reason: As it embraces scientific dis-coveries and rational thinking as complementary to faith, Progressive Liberal Christianity recognizes that science and reason provide valuable insights into understanding the world and encourages critical engage-ment with religious beliefs.

Environmental Stewardship: Because it recognizes the urgency of environmental issues, Progressive Liberal Christianity advocates for responsible stewardship of the Earth. It emphasizes the interconnectedness of all creation and encourages sustainable practices to address climate change, pollution, and environmental degradation.

Relationship with Social Justice: Progressive Liberal Christianity's relationship with social justice is intrinsic and transformative. By embracing the principles outlined above, it provides a theological and ethical framework for addressing social inequalities and working toward a more just and compassionate society. Progressive Liberal Christians see social justice as an essential expression of their faith. Inspired by the teachings of Jesus, they actively confront systemic injustices and advocate for the dignity and rights of all people. They understand that faith without action is incomplete, and social justice becomes the embodiment of their commitment to love, compassion, and liberation. Progressive Liberal Christianity recognizes that social justice is not an isolated endeavor but a comprehensive approach to addressing interconnected issues. It acknowledges the complex web of intersecting oppressions—such as racism, sexism, economic inequality, and discrimination against LGBTQIA+ individuals—and seeks to dismantle these systems of injustice.

The movement actively engages in advocacy and grassroots activism to effect systemic change. Progressive Liberal Christians work alongside marginalized communities, listening to their voices, amplifying their concerns, and supporting their struggles. They participate in movements for racial justice, gender equality, immigrant rights, and environmental activism, recognizing that social justice extends beyond the walls of the church and into the wider world.

Moreover, Progressive Liberal Christianity views social justice as an integral part of spiritual growth and transformation. Its followers believe engagement with social justice issues fosters a deeper understanding of the teachings of Jesus and cultivates empathy, compassion, and solidarity with the marginalized. Through active involvement in social justice initiatives, Progressive Liberal Christians seek to align their lives with their values, manifesting their faith in concrete and tangible ways.

Progressive Liberal Christianity's commitment to social justice is not limited to domestic concerns but extends to global issues as well. It recognizes the interconnectedness of all humanity as it advocates for fair trade, poverty alleviation, and global cooperation. The movement supports humanitarian efforts, promotes human rights, and works toward building peace and reconciliation in conflict-ridden regions.

Progressive Liberal Christianity, with its emphasis on openness, inclusivity, social justice, and engagement with contemporary challenges, offers a transformative approach to faith. It sees social justice as an essential expression of religious belief, rooted in love, compassion, and the pursuit of a more equitable and compassionate world. By embracing the principles of Progressive Liberal Christianity, individuals and communities become agents of positive change, working toward justice, equality, and the realization of a more inclusive and harmonious society.

SOMETHING GREATER

Liberation is about being on a journey, being in a movement.
It is the process of coming into an awareness that there is
definitely a better life for people to be had. Not just for
myself but for all of us. The Church should be part of that.
And where it is not, its not the Church.

— *Rev. Dr. Emilie Townes*, Restoring Relationships

In summary, New Thought, while in the crosshairs of rapidly changing ideas, nonetheless aligned with the movements of social reform, progressive Christian thought, and, above all, was a byproduct of the women's rights era.

Yet by the turn of the century, White men rose to positions of leadership across the movement as the nation was swept up in an era of rapid progress, growth, and prosperity, i.e. the dawn of capitalism. New Thought then attracted a new audience: wealthy businessmen or those who aspired to be so. A new era of "do it yourself" was born. The story changed from what we could achieve together (which included personal healing) to what the individual could achieve alone, where personal healing turned into personal success. The era of rugged individualism was born, and with it, all shades of New Thought once engaged in outer social reform retreated in favor of the self-empowered inner work and outward demonstrations of prosperity and success. This proved a magical combination that had the movement see rapid growth and expansion.

This change in emphasis within the movement of New Thought could easily be viewed as the natural evolution of a movement in relationship with the changing world around it. What began as personal health and social reform turned into personal success as a means to respond and grow within the hyper-capitalistic American consumerism birthed in the 1930s. It was a perfect marriage at the time—America's place as a world power bolstered by the gospel of personal success. Responsibility to the collective fell to the side in favor of purely personal responsibility in a land where the individual was king or queen (but mostly king).

We can release any need to admonish the movement for being what it was—a product of its time and a perfect representation of the streams that flowed into it. But the movement would be best served to remember both its value of evolution and "open at the top" stance as it enters a new era today. Liberation movements call out the past, but they don't demonize it, because liberation is always about where we are going, growing, and moving.

Meanwhile, we must not hold it to what it once was in the midst of another season of rapidly shifting world values and focus. Holmes reminds us that progress is eternal and evolution ever-unfolding in and through us. The consciousness of the movement must seek to embody its own principles and evolve its own expression. Whether you agree with this premise or not, it is clear we are in a new era. Clinging to an individualistic based teaching of personal responsibility, success, and promises of wealth in the midst of a collective groan and cry to address systemic inequity will lead only to a movement out of step with society and isolated to an audience of the privileged.

The alternative is to embrace the evolutionary pull into something greater. Together, we stand on the threshold of infinite potential to contribute to the healing of the planet through the laws of consciousness. Together, we can rise as a people who believe the ultimate goal of life, which as Holmes said in his "Sermon By the Sea" (see Appendix B), "is complete emancipation from discord of every nature—and that this goal is sure to be attained by all."

Liberation is at the heart of all humanity. Rev. angel Kyodo williams put it this way: "Liberation wants nothing but liberation for everyone and anyone else." There is something inside us all that yearns to be free. Despite centuries of humanity creating ways to oppress each other and ultimately ourselves, the hunger to be free remains. Liberation and its call cannot be escaped. It is what Holmes referred to as the "Divine urge to express in terms of freedom."

When we understand the liberation path, we understand that everyone has been oppressed, which is to say, some part of your wholeness has been left out, dismissed, forgotten, and discarded. Whether that was due to systems, structures, behaviors, or beliefs, it is something we all have in common because its part of the human journey. We all have internal operating and controlling paradigms that marginalize some part of our larger and whole self. That does not mean that we need to identify as victims, but rather that we recognize ourselves as sojourners on the path of liberation. It does mean that we need to recognize that the journey of spiritual awakening also requires identifying and releasing the ways in which patriarchy, racism, and capitalism have engrained themselves into our mental programing and are thus roadblocks to our greater good. I believe the principles of New Thought are designed as powerful tools of liberation.

As always, when embracing a larger vision for our lives, we must release all the old thoughts and false ideas that stand in the way. Now we must examine the roadblocks or sacred cows and ultimately work to remove them if we want to embody a liberation theology ethic. And finally, we must set our vision on the principles and guideposts for a Liberation Theology lens applied to not just a New Thought movement but, in true New Thought fashion, from a universal perspective such that other progressive and expanded consciousness teachings may be inspired by them as well. ∞

REFLECTION QUESTIONS

1. If you embrace a liberation theology, how does that affect your daily decisions and actions?

_____

_____

_____

_____

_____

_____

_____

2. Does your chosen place of worship embrace the ideals of liberation theology? How can you strengthen or add to those efforts?

_____

_____

_____

_____

_____

_____

3. Envision a world working seamlessly to better the lives of all. What does that look like to you? How can you contribute to reaching that goal?

_____

_____

_____

_____

_____

_____

_____

_____

_____

_____

_____

_____

_____

_____

_____

_____

CHAPTER 6

RECONCILIATION

*Calling attention to our wounds and to the injustices
we are experiencing brings the whole back into integrity with our
values as a nation for equality, life, liberty and the pursuit of happiness. And in order to come back into integrity with those values,
we must be brave enough to understand the ways we've fallen out
of it and continually call out and courageously speak to the ways
in which we are not living in integrity.*

— Rev. Masando Mike Hiraoka, *Guide for Spiritual Living:
Science of Mind* magazine, March 2019

IDENTIFYING ROADBLOCKS
TO OUR VISION

Having read this far, you can see I have sought to make the case
for New Thought as a liberation theology. And in doing so, we already
dispelled a myth, namely that liberation theology is a closed book with
no new entries. When I first started exploring these ideas, I would, in
various settings, propose the notion that New Thought is a liberation
theology. I frequently received pushback at the mere suggestion. "Oh,
liberation theology," I would hear, "that's a Catholic thing. We can't
use that term." Or, "Oh, that's a Black church/revolutionary thing. We
should not use that term." It was not unusual to hear these responses
and to come across individuals who had a narrow definition of liberation

theology that reflected only what they had been exposed to (i.e. Catholic or Black liberation theology), with little or no awareness that it extends beyond that.

Interestingly, I never encountered African American colleagues, who were almost always people who had some knowledge and history with liberation theology, who then took issue with the case I was making. Instead, they understood the connection and welcomed it.

Hopefully, by now I've made the case that: 1. Liberation theology is a much larger field than previously thought, and 2. New Thought has, at the very least, the capacity to claim a seat at the table. Liberation theology is not a book that opened in Latin America in the late 1960s and closed in the United States in the post-Civil Rights era. It remains open and evolving. Likewise, New Thought is not a book that opened in the late 1800s and closed in 1927 with the publication of *The Science of Mind* by Ernest Holmes.

If you believe, as I do, that there is a case to be made for New Thought as a liberation theology, then likely your mind has begun to stray into considering what roadblocks we must overcome to step clearly into this declaration and fully claim our seat at the table. That's a good thing, because it turns out there are a number of roadblocks. The necessity of this book is evidence of the pushback that the evolution of our teaching continuously receives. We fight among ourselves: How much "social focus" is too much? Whether it's over content in the Science of Mind magazine, or our organizational stance on marriage equality, Black Lives Matter, or any other issue, there is no shortage of diverse and divergent ideas and passions among us.

Struggles of identity, mixed with desperate searches for the "golden key" to church growth and organizational success, kept at bay the greater conversation of who we are in context to where we find ourselves. For too long, navel gazing and finger pointing occupied space where authentic becoming and growing into newness ought to be. Are we an association or a denomination? Are we a central or distributed leadership model? Are we Christian, nondenominational, or spiritual but not religious? Are we a goose or a gander?

Self-amused and occupied with our intellectual gymnastics, we fail to address or acknowledge the most important question facing us: Who are we to the world in which we find ourselves? We could argue that is a difficult question to answer if we first do not know who we are to ourselves. Yet if history has taught us anything, it would be that we are a collection of many things and, as such, need a generous and broad description that allows for both variation and diversity, clarity and cohesion. Does such a unicorn exist? I believe it does: liberation theology.

A theology, by definition, is not a single voice imposing itself on the world, but a collection of voices shaped by and responding to the world. Therefore, a living theology need not worry itself about how best to cling to the words of icons gone by, but rather must follow in the footsteps of deep inquiry and adaptive implementation into the world in which it currently finds itself. In other words, a theology is a living thing, breathing new life into the times it exists in and ever learning from times gone by.

All creative (Christian) theologies come into
being as persons encounter contradictions
in life about which they cannot be silent.

— James Cone, For My People:
Black Theology and the Black Church

We face a cognitive dissonance between the world we see projected every day and the one we wish to affirm, visualize, and imagine. But the solution to this dissonance is not to ignore the world as it is, turn our heads, and pretend we don't see what we see. No! The solution is to enter the world as it is, equipped with our vision and affirmations, and to do what is necessary to bring the world of our vision forth into our experience. This has always been the formula, yet it astounds me to realize how often this approach is rebuked or dismissed as something less than the application of the teaching. Ernest Holmes saw the error of such thinking in his own time and warned against it when he said, "We do not say there are no sick—this will never heal anyone."

When theologians and preachers experience contradictions in life that shake the foundation of the accepted faith of the community, they are forced by faith itself to return to its source so as to interpret faith in a new light and thereby be empowered to struggle against the forces of evil that seek to destroy its credibility.

— James Cone, For My People:
Black Theology and the Black Church

This has always been the way of transformation in New Thought. In every arena of personal expression, we teach the same thing. Don't like your financial status? Arm yourself with the vision of prosperity, and then enter your world with honesty and get to work changing the habits, thoughts, and practices that keep you in a lack mentality. How about relationships? Do you desire a shift or something new? Once again, arm yourself with the vision of your heart's desire, and as you hold it in contemplation, pay attention to what arises in opposition. Examine those points of resistance and challenge them; there you will find the gifts to manifesting more meaningful relationships. What about health? The pattern is the same. Hold the vision of what you want, go to work on the points of resistance in your mind, the healing of which makes the tasks of new habits easier. You see? Transformation never comes from the practice of privileged ignorance. But that's exactly what we have far too much of in our movement today: the privilege of ignorance wrapped in the aloof air of "spiritual practice."

"We just need to focus on our individual consciousness!" is the cry I hear all too often, a statement that from pulpit to parishioner expresses the embodied ignorance of the principle of oneness. Too harsh? I don't think so. Instead, I think the cry of "individual consciousness" is too easy a scapegoat for our collective responsibility in the public square. Here's the thing: There is no individual consciousness outside of the One. And our continued insistence that there is stands in the way of our deeper understanding. When we do this, we fail to see the way in which the One consciousness is expressing as each one, individualized, but not separate from the One. The One does so to experience diversity in Its infinite nature and to remind Itself that It is One through all of Its expressions. When I hear someone defend the idea that its all just "individual consciousness" work that we need to focus on, what I hear is them defending privilege, not principle. We need to come to terms with the uncomfortable truth that it is far easier to uphold the pseudo principled stance that individual consciousness will fix the world's problems than it is to roll up our sleeves, enter into the issues, and examine the consciousness behind them.

The other great guardian of the myths we explore in this chapter is the New Thought axiom that we "teach people how to think, not what to think." The implication here is that each individual is left to their own self-discovery. We teach the tools and principles of consciousness, and individuals decide their own opinions and worldviews. Sounds simple enough, and I grew up with deep reverence for this principled approach that guarded my individual sovereignty (something we'll talk more about in myth #5). The challenge here is that this individualistic mindset, that leaves everyone to the privacy of their own thoughts, smacks of separation and isolation. Defending that inside of a philosophy that teaches oneness is quite the accomplishment, if not a profound hypocrisy. For the record, I quite agree that we cannot dictate what people think, but that does not mean on the collective level (locally and organizationally) we cannot demonstrate positions and values-based engagement on topics in the public square. In fact, I think we should consider the ways in which doing so is, in fact, demonstrating how to think and not what to think. If consciousness is all there is, then the how of any social issue is by the laws of consciousness.

This understanding leads me to the conclusion that we can and should speak more, not less, about social issues. Who else would be qualified to speak to the principles of consciousness behind all that vexes us socially? Unfortunately, we too often are stuck in our own hall of mirrors, convinced we have no voice in the social ills created by principles of consciousness, our self-proclaimed field of expertise. All the while, the world cries out for a better answer to our challenges.

Tensions exist in the New Thought movement because there is a perceived rift between what was once thought of as a tranquil and holistic personal philosophy, practiced by mostly well-off individuals, and its current state of expression that extends far beyond the comfort zone of many of its adherents to address some of the issues faced in the broader world. A real and genuine practice of oneness necessitates a growing awareness of places, conditions, and realities that we have not previously contemplated or needed to consider. In other words, when we awaken to the wider world around us, the shift gets real.

Our teaching flourished in spaces that were vastly protected by systems of privilege, but that is not the same as saying that our teaching is one and the same with those systems. The dynamic and challenging conversations within our walls about the future and direction of our teaching prove this out. The systems and structures of privilege, class, and race are under a microscope by the collective society. Technology, in the form of social media, has given expression to a collective mind or zeitgeist in which old thoughts and systems are questioned, challenged, and, if necessary, dismantled. The question for New Thought is who we are in the midst of this collective reconstruction. What do we have to bring to the table?

Our vision says that we believe in a world that works for everyone. The promise of our teaching is the emancipation from discord of every nature—a goal that Holmes tells us is "sure to be attained by all." If that's true, then stepping into a bold new vision will require releasing that which no longer serves us.

In the life-visioning practice articulated by Dr. Michael Bernard Beckwith, a core spiritual practice of Centers for Spiritual Living, the last questions asked in the process are: "What must be released in order that this vision can come into full view with no obstructions? What must be released or let go of?"

Here are some thoughts that the New Thought movement, in its entirety, must let go of to manifest a world that works for all.

MYTH #1: WE ARE NOT POLITICAL HERE.

The conviction that religion must be
rigorously excluded form political life has been
called the charter myth of the sovereign nation-state.

— *Karen Armstrong, "The Myth of Religious Violence," published*
in the March 10, 2015, issue of Tricycle Magazine

The only faith tradition in the world that conforms to the modern myth that religion should be something codified and private (and separate from public life) is Protestant Christianity, which is itself a product of the modern world. This privatized and commodified notion of religion has infected the Western cultural mindset, and New Thought is not immune to this development. It is not uncommon to hear people defend religion as something that is private and personal. We are trained as children that as we enter adult spaces, we don't talk about the big three—religion, politics, and sex—in public. While it's true that there are individual rights and choices in each area to be defended and protected from public opinion, it is also true that there are profoundly public and collective consequences associated with these topics. Since there are consequences and implications of a collective nature, one may well ask: Who is monitoring or regulating these topics in the name of the public good, especially if you and I can't talk about them? Turns out, while prudence convinced us to remain silent, politicians and religious extremists never stopped talking about them behind closed doors and where policy decisions get made that directly affect our lives, our communities, and our bodies.

The idea that Jesus was apolitical—
just teaching people how to be nice and get
ready for heaven—has been a tool used by empires
since at least the third century to keep Christians'
attention off of the "on Earth" part of the Lord's Prayer.

— Josh Scott, Bible Stories for Grown Ups

If the rise of the religious right, the "moral majority" in the 20th century, taught us anything it is that our value of modesty and low appetite for conflict purchased our silence to the detriment those on the margins. Women, children, LGBTQIA+ youth and adults, health care, our non-Christian faith neighbors, Black and Brown bodies—basically everyone except White men all have been harassed, subjected to policy discrimination and oppressive or prejudicial treatment by the laws of the land.

Let us be clear: The Protestant Christian value that church community space is a tranquil, docile, and politically neutral space that does not speak up or out to challenge the wrongs and inequities of the world is the manifestation of slaveholder religion. When slaveholders forced Christianity onto the enslaved, they did not do so out of altruistic hearts. And they certainly did not do so to help liberate the souls of the enslaved. Slaveholders had little interest in the salvific nature of Christianity when it came to the source of their free labor and, thus, the engine driving their economic power.

Slaveholders were, as it turned out, far more interested in the controlling capacity and social hierarchy that the practice of Christianity gave them. They sought to force the enslaved into a worldview they held for themselves in relation to their understanding of God. The transfer of their Protestant values focused on being meek, subservient, and humble before the Lord—except in this case, the enslaved people's Lord was a substitute for their slave master.

As late as 1800, most of the enslaved in the United States had not been converted to Christianity. In the years that followed, however, widespread Protestant Evangelicalism, emphasizing individual freedom and direct communication with God, brought about the first large-scale conversion of enslaved men and women. At first, itinerant ministers, captivating large audiences at revivals and camp meetings across the North and South during the middle part of the century, reached only a small percentage of the enslaved population with their calls to Christianity.

Whereas an earlier generation of evangelical preachers had opposed slavery in the South during the early 19th century, Protestant clergymen began to defend the institution, invoking a Christian hierarchy in which slaves were bound to obey their masters. For many slaveholders, this outlook not only made evangelical Christianity more palatable, but also provided a strong argument for converting slaves and establishing biracial churches.

— https://www.thirteen.org/wnet/slavery/ experience/religion/history2.html

To maintain the Protestant ethic of church as "neutral ground" in the face of a world rife with injustices is to practice a kind of complicit silence in the face of evil. It is a morally bankrupt position that sentences our teaching to the slow decay and ultimate death of irrelevancy. Responding to this harsh criticism with spiritual platitudes that "there is no evil" may be received well in the pews of privilege, but the argument falls on deaf ears to those on the margins of society whose lives are impacted by the evil and immoral actions of public policy that degrades human dignity. In the Jewish prophetic text, Joel 3:2 says that God will gather all the nations and put them in the valley of judgment. There He will judge the nations for how they have treated His people. In other words, the judgment is evaluated through a nation's public policy, not its religiosity or individual piety.

Yet this task—to combat the myth of political neutrality as a moral standard—like most on this list, is easier said than done. Far too many churches built their reputations and their wealth on being "purple" in a red/blue divided nation. Whole communities coalesced and built their foundations on the practice of "neutral ground" on Sunday mornings. These communities see it as a high value of the culture and community that they do not venture into "politics from the pulpit." There is a real threat to the balance books, mortgage notes, and budgets of churches that pride themselves and historically built themselves on the practice of not rocking the boat when it comes to issues or topics that prove political. To be fair, there is equally a financial cost and risk to the solvency of a community that speaks out on social issues—especially and explicitly because its members have for too long valued the privileged neutrality of their community.

"I don't do politics from the pulpit," ministers announce with pride, accompanied by grateful congregants who nestle into the comfort of a social club rather than a place that challenges and applies their faith to the world around them. But this prideful footing places such spiritual communities on a foundation of quicksand. The body is stable only if you don't look closely. Inch by inch, day by day, those who take this path sink into an immobile position, unable to speak to the pressing issues that confront them, lest they face the wrath of an offended member. Churches are not immune to so-called cancel culture; in fact, they may well be the birthplace of it.

There is an old story that speaks of a man rescued from a deserted island after many years. The rescuers were amazed to find his adaptability and survival skills when they arrived. He gave them a tour, pointing out the hut he used for sleeping, the sheltered space where he cooked and stored food, his workshop for building and repairing his shelters, and a beautiful hut he called his church. Then the rescuers noticed one more hut in the distance. When they asked what was in that hut, the man said, "Oh, that's the church I used to belong to."

Yet, regardless of this perceived high moral stance, the boat continues to take on water. The silence speaks of complicity to conditions that exist because they go unchallenged. The silence speaks violence to members or potential members who identify with marginalized populations that are under attack. This "neutrality" says to them, "You [minister/spiritual community] will not defend my dignity. In fact, you'll explicitly choose silence in the face of my human dignity being degraded, in order to appease the comfortable and privileged among you who are not directly affected but who might otherwise be offended if you mention anything." How is that message empowering to anyone on any side? How do we expect such perceived neutral space to grow in diversity when it's clear that the very diversity we seek will not be defended or protected when under attack by public policy?

What pastors, ministers, and church leaders of all stripes need to hear clearly is this: *Neutrality won't save you.* Dr. Martin Luther King Jr. warned about the silence of White moderates as the largest threat to civil rights for a reason. Congregants who demand neutrality from their ministers are not seeking a principled or moral high ground. They seek sheltered protection from doing their own inner work of wrestling with what it means to be one with those being marginalized. They want to promote oneness without understanding it. They need moral courage and leadership, not compliance in playing small.

Don't get me wrong, many of them will leave if churches change course now, I know that road firsthand, but that is just as much a function of their unwillingness to grow as it is a function of the conditioning these churches have provided, which is to say, if people have not been challenged to grow, look within, and confront their own conditioned assumptions, then jumping in the deep end with a hot button "politicized" issue is more than likely to send them running.

The other thing ministers and leaders need to know is that marketing an exclusive focus on "personal/inner" work will not save their churches. The prosperous days of individual spiritual consumerism are over, and to the degree that there's still money on the table in this space, it is dominated by the personal life-coach market, not by ministry. If you want to be a life-coach and teach personal empowerment principles, then please get out of pulpit ministry, and go do that. Ministry is communal and must speak to the whole community, not a select client base who can afford your coaching fees. Obviously, people turn to ministers for advice, guidance, and even coaching, but if your whole model is a pay-to-play structure, then you have strayed from the calling of ministry that is communal in nature.

The challenge here is one of our own making, and there are two main arteries that continue to feed this cancerous "too political" cell in the church body. The first is that we confuse what is "political" with taking sides, and the second is that we lack training in and a culture of clergy accessing their prophetic voices. These two shortcomings at best hold back our evolution and at worst get held up as virtuous standards of our movement. Both are mistakes we must correct if we wish to move into our potential.

Over and over again, what we fail to understand is that the role of the prophetic voice in spiritual community is not to take sides on political topics but rather to cut through the fake and divisive narratives and bring humanity back to its senses. The role, properly understood, is to snatch from the jaws of political cannibalism the subjects of human dignity, justice, and equality, and place them back on the alter of humanity where they belong.

> *The task of prophetic ministry is to nurture,*
> *nourish, and evoke a consciousness and*
> *perception alternative to the consciousness and*
> *perception of the dominant culture around us.*

— *Walter Brueggemann,* The Prophetic Imagination

The power of theology is the power to expand our imagination, as theology offers the possibility of a prophetic imagination that can transform the individual and society.

— *Mark Charles and Soong-Chan Rah,*
Unsettling Truths: The Ongoing,
Dehumanizing Legacy of the Doctrine of Discovery

You see, the topics of so-called culture wars are topics of basic human dignity: gay marriage, gun control, women's health care, transgender rights, and racial equity. For a pastor, any pastor, to surrender these topics to the jaws of politicization and thus avoid them for fear of alienating one side or the other is to dishonor the basic dignity of humanity itself.

Nevertheless, the New Thought movement should not miss the moment that is before it. A spiritual theology that dares to proclaim a radically inclusive spiritual equality must stand up and speak up in a nation and world where basic human rights are denied to any of its people. Failure to do so is spiritual malfeasance and theologically bankrupt behavior that fails to live up to the principle of oneness it claims to represent. We are political by nature because to be human and live in the context of community is itself a political act.

Political activity is simply activity that governs our collective experience. It's not the taboo and untouchable space separate from that which is spiritual, especially within a theology that claims that God/Divine Intelligence is the source of all that is. How is politics outside of the allness of God? Simple. It's not. Political conversations, topics, and ideas exist within the One Mind common to all humanity and are worthy of the same spiritual investigation and subject to the same laws of consciousness as the topics of individual success, happiness, health, and relationships that so often fill our teaching.

It is that failure to recognize our position within the context of a wider community that vexes us. New Thought's greatest liability is also its greatest asset: teaching liberation to the individual. Coming into an empowered state as individualized expressions is a critical function of spiritual growth, as well as physiological brain development.

Yet our growth cannot stop there. We must also grow in the awareness of our connection to and dependence within community. Our spiritual awakening must include a conscious awareness of the inextricable garment of destiny that Dr. King spoke of.

Those who believe the church and politics
are not connected do not understand either.

— *Mahatma Gandhi*

Years ago, when I was interviewing Bishop Dr. Yvette Flunder for a social justice conference being put on by the Association of Global New Thought, I asked her, "What do you want a New Thought audience to know more than anything?" She said, "I love your people, your teaching, and your affirmative language and view on life. You understand the power of the word, but I need you to start using it. I need you to stop praying as if there are no lives on the line. Beloved lives are on the line everyday. Use what you got to heal that. I need you to stop praying as if there are no lives on the line."

MYTH #2: CONDITIONS (RACISM, SEXISM, ETC.) ARE IN THE CONSCIOUSNESS OF THE PEOPLE EXPRESSING OR EXPERIENCING THEM.

The second issue we need to release and let go of so that the path toward a world that works for everyone is made clear, is the idea that conditions (i.e. racism, sexism, homophobia) are solely in the consciousness of the people expressing and or experiencing them; they are not "in me." This toxic idea comes from its individualized cousin, which says that individuals suffer the consequences of their own consciousness. While it is true that we are each at the effect of our own thinking, it also is true that we do not live in a vacuum. It is important to be liberated from negative self-talk, and it's equally important to be liberated from the toxic notion that we are on an island of our own making, without the impact or influence of both the society at large and the direct community surrounding us. Yes, we can get free from the toxic thoughts and beliefs planted in our subconscious by others, and we must also get free from the idea that we alone created our reality. It is critically important to free ourselves of this because it leads to shame and blame for circumstances not in our immediate control and, when left unchecked, expands our blame to those at the effect of systemic forms of oppression (racism, sexism, etc.).

This is both hurtful and just plain wrong. Giving yourself a free pass and clean slate in consciousness is a spiritual bypass, and shaming others for their experiences, claiming its all due to their own consciousness, whether consciously or unconsciously, is spiritual gaslighting. Full stop. This myth is an extension of its big brother–self-responsibility, which promotes the idea that we are solely responsible for our experiences. This idea seems empowering at first, especially if you come to this idea through the door of victimhood (the idea that life is happening to me). Claiming personal responsibility is a means by which we take "control" of the situation and begin, perhaps for the first time in our lives, to discover the power of our consciousness in directing our thoughts. While our consciousness plays an invaluable role in our interaction with conditions, it is a dangerous oversimplification to state that we solely create or control these conditions.

First and foremost, we are always co-creators, never sole creators, of conditions. This is a distinction that often gets lost in our hyper-individualism language. Conditions, no matter the type, are either co-created, promoted, or allowed. Those are the three ways in which we "create conditions." As co-creators, we remember that we are always working with a law and with conditions, circumstances, and systems that have come before us. Ignoring this truth puts us at great risk of operating under the illusion that we do it all by ourselves, for ourselves, and thus to ourselves. Such illusions separate us from the larger system we are inseparably connected to and a byproduct of.

Second, the only thing we ever really "control" is our state of mind via our reaction to and opinion of the conditions that surround us. While this reaction may spur on new actions that contribute to changing the course of the condition in the long term, it is the reaction and subsequent actions that we are controlling, not the condition itself. Conditions are secondary; state of mind is primary.

Third, we have to make a distinction between individual conditions, like the status of my relationship, health, or bank account, and systemic conditions, like the economy, race relations, and public attitudes toward or about social issues. Racism, sexism, and all the "ism's" of the world are a systemic issue of collective consciousness and exist as an operating culture in society. More importantly, these conditions were not created "over there" by "them." Instead, they were created out of the One Consciousness that is the only consciousness there is, which exists in you and in me as our consciousness, because it is the only consciousness there is. Yes, you and I have our own individualized and unique experiences within consciousness; that said, those experiences are still contained within the One.

To think of it any other way is to participate in separation and division of the One for our own comfort. Let's face it: Practicing oneness is hard. It's much more tempting to claim our safe space from each other when the effects of our fractured sense of oneness begin to reveal themselves. It is so much easier to separate from the ugliness of the world around us and claim that it is all sourced by someone else's misuse of the law. However right that might feel on the micro level, the uncomfortable truth is that the so-called individual misusing the law still is very much connected to us, and is, in a very real way, a reflection of our own consciousness.

Furthermore, we need to stop pretending that seeing and speaking out about a problem is equal to giving it power or creating it. Naming the errant condition at the source of our troubles is essential in the practice of our teaching. The light of our faith helps us see it. It also helps us see both ourselves in it and it in ourselves. Furthermore, the practice of non-judgment would invite us to simply begin to apply our principles to what we see, not blame the one seeing or experiencing the issue. It is only when we get curious, from a space of non-judgment, about the conditions we see that we can begin to see their source.

Those at the effect of racism or other conditions no more created or attracted it to themselves than you or I attracted the weather to ourselves. The collective consciousness of humanity created these conditions. Individuals may amplify and project them, but it is a collective condition they are promoting. And while it's true that if an individualized expression of racism, sexism, etc., comes your way, you have the power and choice to rise above it, ignore it, and not be subject to it on the internal level, it would be a grave mistake to say that any of us, regardless the conditions we experience personally, are not affected by them.

As an individual, I may choose to not be offended if someone calls me a name or discriminates against me in some way. In many ways, a healthy sense of self, pride, and dignity can ward off even the most vulgar acts— the "when they go low, we go high" practice. However, collective effects of racism, sexism, and other prejudiced beliefs impact our politics, taxes, health care, mortgage insurance, and many other aspects of our lives. Simply put, we all are impacted, whether we choose to recognize it or not. In truth, it takes a tremendous level of privilege to uphold the illusion that we are immune to the effects of these conditions. Racism affects us all, as does climate change, as does every other "ism" in the world. Awakening to the power you have to direct your consciousness does not make you special and immune to conditions around you. It makes you responsible for and in relationship to them.

We might conclude that we are all impacted because we are all one, which is correct, but we are impacted at different levels. Some might say we are all in the same boat, but it would be more accurate to say that we are all in the same ocean. Some of us are in large, comfortable cruise ships, with weather radar, on-board hospitals, and gourmet kitchens stocked with food. Others are on small rafts, makeshift dinghies, or small sailing vessels whose sails have been torn and damaged by the winds of injustice.

When the position that these conditions only occur in those who feel or express them is taken and stated toward a Person of Color in our movement, that position creates a form of shaming and blaming that damages everyone involved. As such, we would be wise to be on the lookout for these biased expressions and counteract them with more authentic demonstrations of the tools of consciousness. Failure to do so simply promotes and protects a theology of privilege. Our reconciliation then is between the worlds of our philosophy and our theology.

Every theology is created and shaped by the conditions that surround it. New Thought is no exception to this rule. As such, we can reasonably suspect that Ernest Holmes got some things wrong regarding the great mystical truth of oneness, including his privileged perspective of our power to create our own reality. We have come to understand that the way our teaching is sometimes embraced can actually foster fear-based denial, spiritual bypassing, and magical thinking when it comes to the very real and current suffering in the world.

Indeed, there is no God outside of ourselves. Neither are we outside our oneness with our fellow humans. We believe that by standing with those who suffer and acknowledging their challenges, we take the first steps to healing. At the very least, this is a compassionate place to start. This form of solidarity is a crucial part of liberation theology, as we discussed in Chapter Four.

Because whatever has happened to humanity,
whatever is currently happening to humanity,
it is happening to all of us. No matter how hidden
the cruelty, no matter how far off the screams
of pain and terror, we live in one world.

— *Cole Arthur Riley,* Black Liturgies

MYTH #3: FOCUSING ON THE CONDITIONS PERPETUATES OR, WORSE, ATTRACTS MORE OF THEM.

The Prophets sought to convey: that morally
speaking, there is no limit to the concern one
must feel for the suffering of human beings, that
indifference to evil is worse than evil itself, that in a free society,
some are guilty, but all are responsible.

— *Rabbi Abraham Joshua Heschel*

This myth is pure spiritual bypass, magical thinking based in the law of attraction. It is metaphysical malpractice to continue this line of thinking in our teaching. This overly simplistic practice of focusing only on positive things—and the corollary that focusing on so-called negative things will bring them about—is toxic New Thought theology.

Perpetuating this type of thinking is what I call playing in the shallow end of the pool. If you imagine a large pool at a waterpark, you can see that on one end, the entry is easy. The water is only half-an-inch deep, and there is play equipment for the kids. Other areas are as deep as 3 feet and have steps into them. And at the other end, the water is 15 feet in depth or more, with diving boards or a big wave machine. Our teaching is like this. The water is the same across the entire pool, but the point of entry and the depth of water changes the overall experience in various locations.

When I was younger and in this teaching, I believed this sentiment and practiced it. Just keep focused on the positive, eliminate the negative, and don't mess with Mr. In-Between. As simple as a song and a shape-shifting practice, I thought. At the personal level, all of this can be sound advice. Negative thinking directed at ourselves has proven to be destructive to our mental health and well-being. Yet, this practice has its limitations, and refusing to embrace the shadow side rarely eliminates it. Instead, doing so just suppresses it.

It's one thing to have a practice in which we do not entertain negative self-talk. It's quite another to have a practice where we bury our heads, refusing to acknowledge the conditions around us by refusing to watch the news or giving voice to the struggles of a troubled world, and then claim some pious status or noble practice that is going to save the world. It's not. It is merely privilege masquerading as enlightenment. The end result is toxic positivity. Refusing to see something does not mean that it is not there; it only means that you don't want to look at it.

This seemingly innocuous practice turns sour because it violates the principle of oneness. What do I mean? To claim that these conditions are negative and therefore outside the boundary of my consciousness is a blatant practice of separation. If, on the other hand, oneness is at the center of what I practice, then nothing is outside its boundary. As such, negative conditions are merely conditions that are different from my preference, but still deserving of my conscious awareness, attention, and examination. Perhaps even more so. Furthermore, should we want to say that the collective of humanity has attracted its current negative conditions, we would have to also say that the purpose of doing so was to heal them. Collective or systemic conditions require collective and systemic solutions. Sitting it out because the issue does not affect me personally is not an option. Espousing our oneness is easy; practicing it turns out to be much harder. As Ernest Holmes suggested, abandoning the truth in the hour of our need proves we never knew the truth to begin with.

Dr. Martin Luther King Jr. warned us about this. He said the biggest stumbling block to progress was White moderates who remained silent.

In the face of social conditions that do not reflect a world that works for everyone, an active spiritual practice of ignoring the negative is a practice of blatantly complicit acceptance of such conditions for fear of getting our hands dirty. This brings us to a much deeper revelation: Ignoring the negative is not just shallow and ineffective as a spiritual practice, it's also lazy. It's a far more rigorous and gritty spirituality that insists on its oneness with negative conditions of the world, because such a claim keeps us in relationship to it, and we can only change that which we are in relationship with. When you take the easy way out and dismiss what offends you or that which you do not want to be bothered with, you surrender your power to change it because you cut off the energetic relationship.

In cases of abuse, this is necessary. Yet, too often we are quick to cut off what we still have opportunity to learn and grow from. Relationships are messy, complicated, and filled with nuance. Too often we want a spirituality that is clean, easy, magical, and unencumbered with deep thinking. We've become consumers of pop spirituality rather than practitioners of the transformative tools of consciousness. If we choose the former over the latter, we have to call it what it is: privilege. I'm looking for a community that is unafraid of raw and authentic spirituality.

MYTH #4: BEING COLORBLIND IS SPIRITUAL.

Engagement in social justice work inevitably leads you to look at race relations and how the construct of race impacts everything. Perhaps not surprisingly, this has become one of the biggest areas of serious pushback in my experience. I believe it is because race relations is one of the easiest areas in which we can see the impact of consciousness and, therefore, where we can see how and why New Thought can make an impact. But peeling back the curtain on this area begins to unravel so much of the American story that it can become disorienting for White-identified people. And thus, huge resistance rises up, because people's own identity is at stake.

Race is a social construct. It has no reality in science or the biological make up of humanity. We are 99.999 percent the same on the molecular level. The variations in pigment of skin and physical features we attribute to various "races" make up less than .0001 percent of our DNA. Yet, the social construct of race plays a huge role in the experiences of people on the planet, both individually and collectively. Herein lies a key spiritual principle: that which is spiritually true (ultimate truth) is not always congruent with experience. Yet, just because something is not ultimately true does not mean the experience is not real. We can experience both emotions and conditions (grief, poverty, oppression, depression) that are real and valid in the human condition, even as we acknowledge that they are not true in the ultimate spiritual sense.

So while it is true that we are all one, it is the valid human condition that experiences vary based on how the color of our skin determines, consciously and unconsciously, the treatment we receive. Full and unambiguous acknowledgement of this is critical in a spiritual philosophy that claims both oneness and conscious awareness. Too often the cognitive dissonance that this reality presents is met with a "peaceable solution," seemingly grounded in the principle of oneness: Being colorblind. "I don't see color. I only see God in all people."

Colorblindness as a spiritual practice is one of the biggest lies ever pushed onto our communities. There is nothing spiritual about being indifferent to human experience. In every religion, New Thought included, the fulfillment of the our divine assignment is found in the marriage between spirit and body, heaven and Earth, human and Divine. The power is *and*. We are a teaching of inclusion, not exclusion. We include our humanness. We do not eliminate or ignore it. God made the diverse colors of humanity as beautiful expressions of the One. Why would we ignore them?

The cultural variation and diverse experiences represented by the colors of humanity add beautifully to the experiences and perspectives of life. Saying, "I don't see color," is saying, "I don't see the unique ways and experiences you bring to the table. I don't see how your unique experience brings value to my understanding." Blind, indeed. What an indifferent and aloof position to take. Take that position, if that's what you believe, but don't claim it is spiritual. God does not ask Its creation to be colorblind. God created the colors and requires us to be colorful, color appreciative and sensitive. We literally are wired to see color and to learn from perspectives outside our own.

MYTH #5: THE MYTH OF RUGGED INDIVIDUALISM AND THE PROBLEM WITH SELF-RELIANCE.

America has a problem, a problem deeply rooted in the very fabric and idea of what America is. This problem is embedded in our origin story and pulses loudly through the veins of our cultural identity today. The myth of rugged individualism has long been a defining characteristic of the American psyche. It embodies the belief that self-reliance, independence, and personal determination are the keys to success and prosperity. This myth has deep historical roots, dating back to the early days of American colonization and westward expansion. As such, it also has deep roots in the New Thought movement. However, it is essential to recognize that while the concept of rugged individualism has, for better or worse, played a significant role in shaping the American identity and New Thought philosophy, it is also a myth, one that often obscures the interconnectedness of society and the role of collective efforts.

It turns out that our inter-dependence is just as important as our independence, if not more so. This myth is responsible for a great deal of New Thought's success and popularity, and one may wonder if we rid ourselves of this toxic sense of self, what of New Thought would be left? It is a fair question, one that we'll attempt to answer in Chapter Seven.

The origin story of rugged individualism can be traced back to the early days of American colonization, when European settlers embarked on a perilous journey to establish new communities in the so-called New World. The harsh conditions, uncertain prospects, and the absence of established institutions forced these early colonists to rely heavily on their own resourcefulness and self-sufficiency. The frontier spirit and the ideal of self-reliance were born out of necessity, as these settlers had to fend for themselves in a vast and unfamiliar land. Or at least that's the story we have been told. American history books brim over with stories of this so-called brave individualistic spirit of early European settlers, forging their way out of no way. It is the story those charged with telling it would have us believe.

The idea of rugged individualism gained further prominence during the U.S. westward expansion in the 19th century. Pioneers and frontiersmen, facing the challenges of the untamed wilderness, often are depicted as lone adventurers who conquered the vast and unforgiving landscapes. The Oregon Trail, the Gold Rush, and the settling of the American West reinforced the notion that individuals could forge their destinies through grit and determination.

During this time, the writings of authors like Ralph Waldo Emerson and Henry David Thoreau celebrated individualism and self-reliance. Emerson's essay "Self-Reliance" seemed to suggest the importance of following our inner convictions and living authentic lives, while Thoreau's book *On Walden Pond* detailed his experiment in living a simple, self-sufficient life in the woods. These philosophical and literary works helped shape the intellectual landscape of the United States and further propagated the myth of rugged individualism.

In actuality this westward expansion combined two elements: 1. a bold colonizing mindset, anchored by genocide, justifying an illusion called "manifest destiny;" and, 2. one of the largest government handout programs ever initiated in the form of land grants and financial assistance to so-called settlers. The U.S. government provided immense support to fuel this all-consuming self-important identity of western settlers. Yes, the popular myth of rugged-individualism was a government-subsidized byproduct of our imagination, required by the lie known as manifest destiny. To be clear, none among us are self-made products of our own efforts. While we all control the levers of our own consciousness, efforts, and story, we also are shaped by the roles others play. Someone taught you to read, write, and walk. Someone believed in you and gave you a chance. Someone created the conditions where the story called "you" could be possible.

We see that the importance of individualism in terms of success, happiness, prosperity, and achievement is central to the Western consciousness, the development of the United States, and to New Thought, the religion of "heathy (individual) mindedness." It can be challenging to separate one from the other, as is evident in the personal nature of the body of literature known as New Thought writings. The writers speak generously to the individual and the quest for personal health, prosperity and well-being through the application of spiritual tools, such as meditation, affirmations, and affirmative prayer. In studying New Thought, we come to the awareness that through alignment with a power greater than you are, the attainment of greater good is not only possible but is our birthright, and that above all else, you should come to a place of believing in yourself, the power of your word, and the essence of God within.

The Problem with Self-Reliance: Many lay the blame for the self-righteous "me and mine" consciousness that infects our society at the feet of America's apostle of self-importance: Ralph Waldo Emerson. After all, Emerson's towering intellectual status, fiercely independent mindset, and bold encouragement of disrupting the status quo and listening to your inner guidance are as American as apple pie and baseball. His writings, particularly his essays, lectures, and poetry, left an indelible mark on the American psyche, shaping how we see ourselves, our place in the world, and our relationship to nature and society. His concept of individualism, as articulated in "Self-Reliance," significantly influenced the American identity. He championed the idea that each person possesses a unique and valuable inner self, and true fulfillment can only be achieved by embracing our individuality and following our inner convictions. This emphasis on individualism has been central to the American ethos, fostering a culture that celebrates personal freedom, autonomy, and self-expression. In other words, in the burgeoning American landscape, the spring waters of individualism seem to bubble up at Emerson's feet and flow into a raging river that carves the landscape for generations to come. As Emerson himself said, "It is said to be the age of first person singular."

In his essay "Self-Reliance," Emerson stated, "To believe your own thought...that is genius. Trust thyself; every heart vibrates to that iron string. Whoso would be a man, must be a nonconformist." He believed that conformity to societal norms and expectations stifles individual potential and creativity. Emerson's promotion of nonconformity encouraged Americans to challenge the status quo, question authority, and seek their own paths. He is, without question, a champion of individual thought and freedom, albeit often taken out of the context of his time and superimposed onto our own to serve our own ends. Such is the lot of icons: Everyone wants to claim them for themselves and use their voices to justify their own positions. Emerson's writings and even our biographical idea of who he was have proven to be malleable to competing doctrines and ideas over the years.

An empowered and liberated sense of self was indeed a key element in the ethos of Emerson's work and worldview. Yet it is misleading to equate it with today's forms of toxic individualism, capitalism, and personal freedoms above all else.

Wesley T. Mott's contribution to *A Historical Guide to Ralph Waldo Emerson* describes him as a "cracked mirror reflecting a conflicting culture's split personality. This should perhaps come as no surprise, for critics have long observed that readings of Emerson typically reflect his reader." For many, Emerson is who they need him to be, which leaves us with diverse and often contradictory conclusions.

Herbert Hoover, in his run for president in 1928, popularized the phrase "rugged individualism," which he framed as a choice between that and a European philosophy of paternalism and state socialism.

This spirit of nonconformity drove many American movements, from the transcendentalism of Emerson to the counterculture of the 1960s, all the way to today's anti-government pushback against individual "sovereignty."

New Thought literature became a welcome fuel feeding the fire of the American Ideal – the mythological self-made man. Henry Ford is said to have used New Thought teachings in his weekly speeches to his employees, and he was personally responsible for thousands of book sales from New Thought authors, which he distributed to his workers. Ford is a highly problematic individual, whose antisemitic views were widely known. Nevertheless, it is easy to see how a self-made "bootstraps theology" was fueled by New Thought literature, principles, and ideas.

Yes, it seems America has a problem, and Emerson is at the epicenter. Yet the problem is not Emerson's ideas. It's not his writing or his encouragement of reliance on our inner guidance. No, the problem is our reading and interpretation of Emerson's work. You see, Emerson, unlike any other American author before or since, holds such an important space in our collective psyche that his body of work takes on epistle-like status. Emerson's is the only work I know, aside from the Bible itself, where I can teach a class and have students with different editions of his essays quote completely different text from the same paragraph. Emerson, like the gospel writers and those of other sacred texts, often is interpreted through our current lens, and this includes the editors of the various publications as well. Whole sentences have been removed or placed in different locations. Sometimes we see the beginning of a sentence magically become the ending and visa versa in competing versions. The only other place I know where this kind of liberty with editing and interpreting takes place is the Bible. Emerson's work serves as a gospel text to American identity. As such, his work has to be interpreted carefully and contextually.

The truth is, Emerson did not promote the kind of rugged individualism we see today, nor that which Herbert Hoover spoke to American voters about. Emerson is not the inspired source of anti-government/establishment or anti-science rhetoric. Emerson is not the celebrated author of independent "bootstraps" philosophy or political ideology, though he can be cited in support of all the above. Emerson and his concept of self-reliance are actually the antidote to all of that.

To understand Emerson's "Self-Reliance," we have to contextually understand the backdrop against which he spoke. Otherwise, we just cherry pick quotes out of context to fit our own narrative, a practice equally dangerous in the Bible as it is in Emerson. Emerson lived in and through a critical and especially turbulent time in American history. Born in 1803, his early life was mired in cultural and socio-economic turmoil. As Samridhya Moitra explains in his article, "Emersonian Individualism and Buddhist Philosophy," "Successive economic booms and busts, the passage of inhuman and discriminatory legislation like the Indian Removal Act of 1830 and the Fugitive Slave Law of 1850, among several others, escalated socio-cultural and interracial tensions, epochal changes stemming from rapid strides in industrialization and urbanization.... The cumulative effect of all these had debilitated the American spirit."

It was these tensions and forces on one side and the burgeoning desire for a responsible alternative to the religious dogma, superstition, and oppressive expression of Calvinistic and Puritan theology on the other that pushed Emerson into uncharted territory to explore both the inner dimensions of self and soul and the inextricable connection to nature and the world on the outer. Here with the rapid modernization of urban spaces, factories, and collective society on one hand, and the westward expansion and eternal longing for freedom from factory smoke and the mad pace of the city on the other hand, Emerson went to work to articulate a new understanding of self and society and our relationship to the Divine. Emersonian self-reliance was not a defense of individualism; it was an antidote to it.

In his two-volume work, *Democracy in America,* which he wrote after a nine-month journey through the United States in 1831-32, French aristocrat Alexis de Tocqueville articulates the dangers of American individualism, describing it as "a calm and considered feeling which disposes each citizen to isolate himself from the mass of his fellows and withdraw into the circle of family and friends; with this little society formed to his taste, he gladly leaves the greater society to look after himself. ... Individualism at first only dams the spring of public virtues, but in the long run it attacks and destroys all the others, too, and finally merges in egoism."

Tocqueville's observations and ultimately scathing analysis exposes America's greatest myths and lays bare the cognitive dissonance of the country's self-image. The self-made independent spirit of the American White male psyche was wholly and utterly dependent on structures of racial hierarchy, control, and submission. Not much has changed.

As professor Jack Turner points out in *Awakening to Race: Individualism and Social Consciousness in America,* "For the individual to see himself as free, independent, and self-sufficient, he had to blind himself to the ways he needed white supremacy for self-confidence and psychic stability.... . Tocqueville's work illuminates not only the particularly individualistic anxieties that promote American white supremacy, but also the peculiarly individualistic cognitive mistakes that facilitate it."

Emerson understood the dangers of the individualism that Tocqueville observed and warned against. At the same time, Emerson and his transcendentalist sojourners marveled at humanity's capacity for autonomy and became unashamed advocates of free thinking. Nonetheless, they understood that, as Turner states, "individuals live in inescapable webs of interdependence and that personal power is socially contingent." It would be pure folly to hold Emerson to any other account.

Emerson and his counterparts, particularly Henry David Thoreau, were reminded daily of the social interdependence their work required.

Thoreau's promotion of the virtues of solitude was wholly dependent on the grace and generosity of Emerson, whose own capacity to "live free" of society's demands came from the wealth he inherited from his first wife. Power, privilege, and class all played significant roles in creating the social context for their "free-thinking lifestyle" and calls for nonconformity.

Yet it was not the transcendentalist who pushed the myth of the self-made man on our nation's psyche. That came, as author of *Bootstrapped: Liberating Ourselves from the American Dream* Alissa Quart points out, from Kentucky Congressman Henry Clay in a speech he gave to the U.S. Senate in 1832, describing the "autonomy of our manufacturers."

From Henry Clay to Henry Ford to Herbert Hoover, we see that the myth of the self-made man was, and still is today, a political invention, not a theological one, an idea that nevertheless used theology to bolster its claim and further legitimize its place in our national psyche.

Despite how his words have been twisted and used by those advocating a mythological creature known as the self-made man, Emerson knew better. Emerson understood that anyone claiming to be wholly independent and self-made should have a conversation with their mother. Emerson heaped praise on his friends, social connections, and those he surrounded himself with for making him a better person. Such were the friends of the Transcendentalist Club, whose free exchange of ideas and mutual support of each others' work cultivated a deeper sense of both the individual self and the larger spiritual Self within. Pressed upon by his Unitarian background and spiritual leanings, Emerson understood there to be a universal side to the self, accessed through the cultivation of a deep listening practice, an inner-reliance that led to a larger connection of human compassion and understanding—a universal Self.

The transcendentalists believed that one of the demands of being an inwardly reflective individual was acknowledging social relations and taking responsibility for social debts. The social and the inner were forever bound and connected through reflection. In other words, learning to rely on this inner wisdom and guidance would lead to playing part in the healing of social ills. Self-reliance did not mean being an island of independent freedom, cold and indifferent to the needs of others, but rather deeply connected to that inner-something that was common to all.

Thus we can see that a deep and contextual dive into the works of Emerson will teach us that individuals live in the context of community and that theology, by definition, is about community.

Philosophy is personal, theology is communal.

— *James Cone*, Black Theology, Black Power

As long as we insist that our teaching is only relevant at the personal level, we will remain impotent to address social ills and, as a result, increasingly irrelevant. It's not that personal success, achievement, and empowerment work is no longer important. Quite the opposite. Such work is as important as it ever was or has been. But the work of personal development must occur in tandem with social and community work. Failure to recognize this fact positions our teaching in a posture of private good, a position defined by privilege. It is time for us to enter the age of first person plural. As the saying goes, "None of us are free until all of us are free." ∞

1. Take a moment to reflect on your positions of privilege. What identities do you associate with? What identities do others associate with you? How do these identities provide or deny access to power and privilege in society?

_____

_____

_____

_____

_____

2. How do you find the balance between inner work and social responsibility?

_____

_____

_____

_____

_____

_____

3. How do you navigate the space between politics and spirituality?

_____

_____

_____

_____

_____

_____

4. How has the politicization of topics helped or hindered our capacity to address them?

_____

_____

_____

_____

_____

_____

_____

_____

CHAPTER 7

FINDING THE FIFTH KINGDOM

*I think that Christianity as a force might have
effectively and lustily survived if it had not for
centuries so notoriously forgotten the teaching of
its own founder. What will take the place of dogmatic Christianity
I cannot guess. But I have a conviction that whatever it is, if it is
not based on kindliness, it will fail.*

— *Anold Bennett*, My Religion

I've described this book project as a love letter from me to the movement I love and have dedicated my life to. It certainly is just that and hopefully a bit more—a vision of what is possible. Looking back on the movement as a whole, we see three distinct eras or waves. While there may, in fact, be more nuanced defining moments for the various organizations under the umbrella of New Thought, taken as a whole, we can see three waves.

The first is defined by the first thirty to forty years. Anchored in the healing practice and methodologies of Phineas Parkhurst Quimby, the movement spread and coalesced into dozens of women-led organizations, schools, magazines, and churches. From San Francisco to Chicago to Denver, Boston, and Los Angeles, women held in their hands the rapid rise and spread of New Thought. As such, the movement was firmly planted in two realms: personal healing and social reform, though the latter is often forgotten or dismissed.

By the late 1920s and early 1930s, New Thought and the thrust of its ideas were primarily, though not exclusively, in the hands of men. This era in America brought a greater emphasis on industry, business, booming urban centers, and a collective focus on capitalism. New Thought found a new audience that flocked to its teachings seeking the keys to personal success, prosperity, health, and well-being. The era of manifesting was born.

By the 2000s, the movement began to shift again, marked by slow and deliberate efforts to heal divides and by slow and cautionary steps toward addressing social issues.

I believe we now are preparing for the fourth wave/shift. This shift already is underway and includes efforts to position our teaching for the 21st century and beyond. This must include modernizing our language to express the principles of New Thought in terms that reach beyond the 19th and 20th century understandings of science, consciousness, and humanity. This includes moving beyond binary constructs, such as "cause and effect" and "male and female" and "either/or" thinking. We believe in a God or Intelligent Source that is bigger than any definition we ascribe. Therefore, our definition must expand. Breaking out of binary thinking is just one form that the deconstruction of New Thought can and must take.

I believe seeing our teaching through the lens of liberation theology will go a long way in supporting this effort. Of course, the task at hand is more than just a new view or vision; there is also some heavy lifting we must engage in. True to New Thought principles, we must take a macro/micro or "as above so below" approach. In other words, we must embody and practice what we teach regarding a liberating mindset. Thus, if we wish to stand for the principles of liberation applied to the human condition, not only does that have a personal and social component, it must have an internal one was well.

In other words, the organizations and institutions of New Thought must liberate themselves of the practices and consciousness that stand in the way of the vision we hold. We must liberate or uncolonize* our institutions of the consciousness of Whiteness, patriarchy, sexism, racism, homophobia, transphobia, and any other "dis-eased" form of consciousness that found its way into our systems and structures. I would suggest that the first step toward this effort is to liberate ourselves from the privileged position of thinking we may be immune to any such thinking because we personally believe it to be incompatible with our principles. If a form of thinking exists in the collective milieu of consciousness in which the organization exists, then some form of the same thinking exists in the organization.

Our organizations were thus not immune to the rampant racism and patriarchy of the 20th century, as evidenced by the male-dominated, capitalistic takeover in the 1930s of what was a women's liberation movement. This deconstruction process is essential in allowing a new vision take place. It is akin to removing the dead weeds and old growth from a garden to make room for the life-giving growth of spring to take hold.

In the previous chapters, I laid out the case for New Thought as a liberation theology, beginning with the premise that all religions take a position on the topic of justice, highlighting the activist and socially concerned roots of our tradition, and casting New Thought development in light of the principles and core values of liberation theology broadly. Yet at the end of the day, the decision of whether or not New Thought takes its place among the traditions of liberation theology is not up to me, no matter what I have written. No one knows that better than me. The decision lies in the collective of those to whom it is entrusted, and it will be dependent on our collective ability to catch the vision of what is possible in a liberation-framed teaching and our collective will to do the decolonizing and internal work.

While I can't offer any guarantee as to where the movement will go, I can lay out my vision and preference. We are each the authors of where things go from here. The story is one we will write together.

In Chapter Two, I discussed how every story has a beginning, a middle, and an end. In this case the "end" is also known as the vision, which points to where we are going and helps inform how we will get there. In keeping with that template, in 2011, Centers for Spiritual Living articulated its vision of creating a world that works for everyone. Similarly, Unity Worldwide Ministries vision is: A world powerfully transformed through the growing movement of shared spiritual awakening. Other spiritually minded organizations speak to the "kin-dom" of radical justice and radical welcome. As we begin with the end in mind and articulate our version of who we wish to become, that vision will begin to inform a doing that is not currently within our reach. In other words, it will form the middle of the story. But first we must have the end in mind. We must answer the existential question: Where are we going? Who do we want to be in a world awakened and working for everyone?

Is our answer one of personal development only, wherein the responsibility of Christ/Atman consciousness remains with the individual alone? If so, then the quest is for self-actualization via the application of the principles of mindful awareness, crafted use of consciousness, and personal dedication toward living our best life. On this path, there is no need to fill churches, except as a means to gain the tools we need for the journey, after which we then leave. The result of this approach is a revolving door of church membership that perpetually declines as the tools and resources become available in other places. For many, this is exactly the experience they have right now. There is no need to support a larger organization or spend any undue amount of energy or time or money on anything other than ourselves in the quest for spiritual self-mastery.

Or is our answer one in which personal development plays an integral part but is by no means the sole path of actualizing our vision? Instead, do we offer a path wherein personal development is just the beginning, coupled with the collective practices of living out our vision? Does our path include speaking up and defending our neighbor when necessary? Do we call for and seek public accountability for the measurable standards of a world that works for everyone? In other words, is justice integral to our own good and our vision of a world that works for everyone? What, in the words of theologian Paul Tillich, is our "ultimate concern"?

How we answer this question, now and in the future, determines the essence of our framing story. At first, the choices seem at odds with each other. We see this dynamic friction expressed in the current diverse responses to the challenges of social justice issues our communities face. Some choose a principled "inner path" of quiet yet firm and resolute confidence that holding space for a better world is an inwardly focused job. Those who choose this path often face pressures for visible public support and visible action, to which they respond, "I don't do politics." Here on this path of the inner mystic, changing the world begins and ends with changing themselves. This inner commitment is deep and profound as we begin to turn from the world of effects toward the deeper, more subtle energies of that which is cause and source of all things external, separation from Source/God. Thus, in this model, the internal reunification to that Source, thereby healing the separation, is the primary and most essential goal.

"There cannot be peace in the world until there is peace within," proponents of this path assert. They will tell you that the greatest contribution you can make to social ills of the world, like poverty, is to be free of the mentality that produces the problems. Thus, in the case of poverty, learning the principles of prosperity, practicing them, and demonstrating them is the best thing we can do to combat this social issue.

So it goes with the rest of the list of social ills. Simply learn to be the best version of you that you can be, free from judgment, projection, bad habits, and negative thinking. Admittedly, that is a lifetime assignment. To back their claims, proponents of this path have the mystics on their side, from Lao Tzu to Buddha to Jesus.

If you want to awaken all of humanity, then awaken all of yourself. If you want to eliminate the suffering in the world, then eliminate all that is dark and negative in yourself. Truly, the greatest gift you have to give is that of your own self-transformation.

— Lao Tzu

Here's the thing: They are not wrong. Individual mindset is crucial to any path of transformation. Holmes said it this way: "The greatest discovery of my generation is that a human being can alter his life by altering his attitudes of mind." It has been said that hurt people hurt other people and that the pain inflicted on the world comes from the unhealed internal wounds of those doing the most damage. Therefore, dedication to the internal healing of all wounds is a profound gift to the healing of the planet and aids in advancing the state of humanity.

Yet this dedication to an inner and personal path should not come at the sacrifice of social engagement or concern. This is the risk of hyperindividualism that Alexis de Tocqueville warned us of in 1835. And in many ways, we already see the full manifestation of the dangers of toxic individualism. In the January/February 2024 issue of The Atlantic, writer Tom Nichols documents how the growing threat to democracy (and social cohesion) comes not from external forces beyond our borders, but from a hyper-individualism within our own. If you take the warnings of Alexis de Tocqueville, add in a heap of disenfranchisement, and feed it strategic misinformation online and in the media, all against the backdrop of a nation that refuses to do deep healing and reconciliation work along racial lines, you then face the toxic and polarized state of American politics today.

It's easy to be overwhelmed by the challenges of the world. Even the most caring among us, the most empathetic get tired and worn out from time to time. It is understandable then to respond by pulling back and coming to the conclusion that all I can do is my own work. I can't change the world, I can only change myself. Therefore, the appeal to the mystical (internal work) path is strong.

But the risk of the mystical path is appearing tone-deaf or, worse, actually being tone-deaf in the midst of social chaos. Saying "I don't do politics" in the midst of a culture war of political issues may seem like a fine way to stay on the sidelines. It sounds and actually is incredibly aloof, privileged, and disengaged. Those whose lives, dignity, and personhood are at stake hear an unspoken message that says, "I don't take a side when your humanity and dignity are brought into question."

As we explored in Chapter Six, the desire for churches to hold politically neutral ground is more a holdover practice from slave-holder religion than it is a best practice of Western Christianity. Further, this position communicates far more than it intends to those on the margins—people of color, LGBTQIA+, or those who may be in the crosshairs of political fire before long. This stance says, in essence, that we don't see you or value your life. Yet we want to be a so-called neutral place so that for those whose personhood is not the subject of legislation or expressions of hate, rather than the dispossessed, can feel comfortable in church. This idea of of church culture is sounding more mythical than mystical, more selfish than selfless and service oriented.

Moreover, the path of the mystic requires privilege. Yes, the mystic is privileged. I define privilege here simply as the freedom from urgency and the abundance of resources. When you are flush with resources and free of the constraints of deadlines, then you exercise privilege. It's easy, for example, to teach prosperity classes in Beverly Hills, but what do we say to those who can't afford market-rate rent or whose home is valued under market value due to the unconscious bias of the appraiser? The realization that there are social forces, held in place by the same laws of consciousness, that impact our individualized experience is something New Thought teachings need to be more aware of and sensitive to. We must come to the realization that citing the "law of attraction" is a wholly inadequate and inappropriate response to systemic injustices. The citizens of Jackson, Mississippi, did not attract dirty and unsanitary water to their homes. Rather, a decades-long broken, racist political system created the conditions of supplying their homes with contaminated water. Systemic problems and injustices require systemic solutions, not the pithy prose of personal responsibility that absolves us of our call to act.

Nevertheless, personal development is important, and New Thought has made a sizable contribution to lifting people out of dogmatic, shame-based religion into positive self-worth and empowered living. So while I don't think this path is wrong—far from it, in fact—I also do not think it is complete. This distinction gets at the heart of the challenge facing the New Thought movement. What we are in the midst of is not a battle of which way to go, it is not a push toward more social engagement versus a pull toward the "old ways." This is not a political versus principle conflict. Furthermore, thinking of this challenge in such terms only keeps the conflict alive, rather than resolving it. To resolve the tensions we feel, we have to seek a both/and approach rather than an either/or conflict.

An inclusive approach leads us to both/and. An inclusive approach has us embrace our social roots *and* our personal responsibility. To find resolution, we need go no further than into the foundational principle of all New Thought: *God Is All.*

If it is true in practice and in theory that God is all there is, then there is no conflict between an inward, personal-focused teaching and an outward, demonstration-focused one. God is not this *or* that; God is this *and* that. Additionally, God is infinitely expressing and evolving. God is not static or polarized. God is the both/and, forever pushing forward into new expressions that move us beyond (but inclusive and honoring of) our traditions.

With these truths anchored in our minds, we can return to the central question: What do we offer in our vision of a world that works for everyone? I would suggest that we offer a both/and God, rather than an either/or one. In other words, the premise is not either you get involved in social issues or you don't, but rather it is doing both the inner work of personal transformation and defending the dignity of your neighbor—and doing so is a demonstration of the inner work you have done.

Of course, to what degree you express commitment to the outer work is still a personal decision, for which there is no right or wrong answer. During the Civil Rights Movement, leaders often reminded those who gathered to get involved, that the movement needed people doing many different kinds of engagement, much of which would not be visible. Those marching and doing sit-ins would need sandwiches. Someone would need to "feed the movement," the saying went.

An integrated (both/and) approach puts us in a relationship with the world around us as it evolves, expands, and contracts in its collective expression of God consciousness. Just like the relationship we have with our own personal journey and development, we come to understand there is a reason it is called spiritual practice.

FINDING THE FIFTH REALM

Most people in our movement are familiar with the "four kingdoms of consciousness." This model, popularized by the works of Michael Bernard Beckwith and referenced in secular works, such as *The 15 Commitments of Conscious Leadership: A New Paradigm for Sustainable Success* by Jim Dethmer, Diana Chapman, and Kaley Klemp.

This model has proven effective in describing the paradigms our minds operate in, evolve through, and sometimes get stuck in, as well as highlighting the key spiritual lessons we must learn to move from one paradigm to the next. In an an effort to contribute to the evolving and expanding consciousness of the movement in more inclusive and liberating language, I refer to the "kingdoms" as realms of consciousness going forward. Each realm has a gateway or key insight that conscious awareness must obtain before it can move to the next realm.

Realm One: TO ME

"Life is happening to me." This is the construct from which most people in our modern American culture operate most of the time. Here we feel the world happens to us. This is the realm in which we are emotional victims, i.e., we blame others for how we feel, expect others to make us feel special, become angry and resentful when others do not meet our perceived needs. At best, playing the victim offers relief from being responsible for making poor decisions, engaging in toxic relationships, having agency in the outcomes of the world. At worst, it leads to severe depression, suicidal ideation, even violence.

Ultimately, though, it leaves people feeling powerless, including those who masterfully gain attention from this state of consciousness. Everyone in this state of mind seeks a way out.

The gateway out of "To Me" is learning and embracing self-responsibility over victimhood.

Realm Two: BY ME

"I am in control of the world." This is the realm in which people start to realize they have some agency and responsibility for their experiences. We see a lot of people in the self-help field on this level seeking to "manifest" external outcomes and success. People at this level of awareness learn how to consciously direct emotions, thoughts, and feelings. When we gain so-called control or mastery of these faculties, we begin to see the attraction of new experiences. Thus, this realm often is referred to as the manifesting realm.

This is definitely a step up from the victim narrative in level one, yet trying to control life's circumstances is ultimately a trap. It is the ultimate spiritual paradox that we must learn to become masters of our senses, thoughts, and emotions, and yet we must learn to surrender to something bigger than we are. Therefore, the gateway out of "By Me" is learning surrender over control.

Realm Three: THROUGH ME

"I am a vessel for Spirit." This is the realm where we learn to lean into a power greater than we are. In this realm, we put aside the need to be victims, the need to be in control, and instead practice a rational faith. "I'm just here to serve," captures this essence. We practice self-care, gratitude, connection with a Higher Power, and then we use that energy to decide where to go, what to do, who to talk to, what to say, how to act and react.

It is from the space of "God moves through me" that we can make clear-headed decisions, take on new responsibilities, and connect with others in mutually rewarding ways.

The gateway out of "Through Me" is seeing our greater oneness over any lingering sense of separation.

Realm Four: AS ME

"I am One with God and all beings." This is the immersion people often describe at the peak of an intentional drug trip, during deep periods of meditation, or even during intense sexual connections. It is a complete loss of the individual physical identity and joining into pure energy. It can be incredibly rewarding, but not sustaining. It is said of this level, "Eventually, you'll need to come back to Earth to use the bathroom."

As ecstatic and transforming as this level is, it is limited because it is experienced strictly at the individual level. Paradox enters in again as you experience oneness, yet the experience happens at the individual level. We can easily become addicted to chasing this ecstatic state of consciousness on purely individual terms, without regard for or mutual concern to the collective.

Therefore, the gateway out of "As Me" is reaching a deeper sense of mutuality, versus staying stuck in what would otherwise become toxic individualism.

CREATE THE FIFTH REALM: AS WE

The Four Kingdoms model has been an immensely valuable tool for countless sojourners in their quest for a spiritually enlightened existence. That said, as we look at what our framing story will be for the 21st century and beyond, I believe we need to critically examine foundational models such as this one so we can honor our own principles of being an evolving teaching.

While this model is not linear—meaning we do not move in a straight line from one realm to the next but rather bounce from one to the other in random patterns—there is nevertheless the desired outcome to live our lives primarily from the second and third realms, with occasional visits to the Fourth Realm as the peak of mystical awareness/consciousness. This trajectory is perfectly consistent with a path of personal development. However, as a means to contribute to the vision of a world that works for all, I find it stops short of a truly transformational contribution. If personal enlightenment is the goal, then the four realms model works fine. But, as I've often said of spiritual work, if you were meant to do it alone, you'd be the only one here.

Community is an inherent element of spiritual development. I think it's time to add to the model. It's time for a Fifth Realm: AS WE. The Fifth Kingdom of Consciousness is where our personal enlightenment leads us to the collective, to the all-ness of God as humanity. Theologian and mystic Howard Thurman reminds us that you cannot love humanity, because love is intimate and humanity is generic. You can love Linda or John as individualized expressions of humanity, but not humanity in general. You must get specific in the application.

This Fifth Realm of Consciousness seeks to apply the principles and practices gained in the struggle to break out of victim thinking and live in a deeper mystical awareness, even if briefly, to the whole of society as an affirmation of our awareness of our oneness. Gone is any sense of "I got my enlightenment; you go get yours." And in its place is a sincere desire to serve humanity in specific and tangible ways.

As such, in the case of the example of poverty I offered earlier, it is not enough to practice the principles of prosperity in our own lives (yet notice that it still is important). In the Fifth Realm, we move beyond our own personal success and claiming of good, and we seek to ensure that the policies, practices, and systems in place focus on the financial liberation of all peoples, not just ourselves. This is similar to the AA community, in which a person's own sobriety is not complete without the twelfth step, in which they are in service to the liberation of others as they begin their journey. Thus, adding the Fifth Realm of "As We" allows the cycle of what started as personal growth and development to come full circle in servitude to all of humanity.

> *The ultimate aim of the quest must be neither release nor ecstasy for oneself, but the wisdom and the power to serve others.*
>
> — *Joseph Campbell*, The Power of Myth

BUILDING THE FIFTH REALM TOGETHER

> *We are all parts of one indivisible whole, which love and suffering reveal. And while we come apart from time to time, while we push each other away in fear, the natural resting position of life on Earth is to join, so that we can release the lifeforce inherent in the biological, societal, and mystical fact that the whole is greater than the sum of its parts.*
>
> — *Mark Nepo*, More Together Than Alone

Every movement must build for and toward its future, while honoring the foundation its founders laid. A balance must be struck between honoring the past and using it as a foundation to build toward something new. I believe a New Thought movement of the 21st century and beyond must make room for both the powerful inner work of the mystic and the community and social engagement of the activist, where the principles and values of our theology are made visible to the world. Building an inclusive movement together must begin with the principle of inclusion.

Here at the intersection of the mystic and the activist is where our work is. The activitst seeks to make real the world that works for everyone by ensuring that systems and structures are equitable, fair, and just. The mystic seeks to know this is not just possible, but that it is already so in the Mind of God, because in spiritual reality, all is one. The mystic seeks to live from the inner conviction of oneness, despite any condition or circumstance that would say otherwise.

Mysitic David Steindl-Rast said that mystic traditions and religions die in politics—which is to say that the capacity to see all things as one dies in the realm of politics, where labels, resources, and separation loom large. Yet, politics and its illusion of separation also is the space where activism is born. Activism is born when the spark of the mystical truth of our oneness is ignited and carried forth by champions. An inclusive spiritual tradition must make room for both the mystic and the activist.

While politics is the space that governs the shared resources and story of humanity, it also is the place where mysticism and activism live on polarized but balanced ends of an infinity loop.

Our movement, in its infinite inclusivity, ever expands the table, ever makes room for more. If the table is inclusion, then the meal is liberation, and proper recognition to the sources of all the elements on the table must be given honor. There is room at our table for the mystic who wishes only to turn within and know the truth with such depth and conviction that it cannot be denied. There is room at our table for the activists, compelled by their vision to move their feet and make real their values. There is room at our table for the prophet, who, in speaking truth to power, knows how to affirm our possibilities while calling out those who violate the human dignity and worth of any of our siblings. There is room at our table for the conscious activist, who skillfully blends the art of affirmative prayer with political organizing and prophetic vision, a casting that calls all to the table to do the work.

There is room at our table for the hungry and the well-fed. There is room at our table for the broken hearted and the blissed out. There is room at our table for praise to and honor for the sources of our inspiration that extend beyond 20th century White men. The table we set can and must honor African and Indigenous spirituality as specific sources of our ancient wisdom, while inviting new voices to the table.

EXPANDING OUR TENT OF CONTRIBUTORS

In the early and burgeoning days of the New Thought movement, the label "New Thought" became a gathering place for voices that broke paradigms and boundaries in their respective corners and institutions.

There has never been a single central authority to define New Thought, only movements with more or less popularity and traction than others at any given moment. New Thought has been both a direct source of inspiration for contributors and social reformers and an open tent whose footprint expands as people practice the tenets of the teaching in their own ways.

Unity and Religious Science/Centers for Spiritual Living have been dominant organizational entitles in this 150-year history. Even so, neither has been the sole arbiter of what is or is not considered New Thought.

All human institutions have a valid self-preservation interest in their expression. Yet this fact should not blind New Thought organizations from limiting how the movement is being shaped today or who is doing the shaping. The unique challenge to the institutions of New Thought remains that what they seek to promote, protect, and preserve is a set of principles, consciousness, and spiritual ideas that are bigger than the efforts to define them. Therefore, if we must build boundaries to identify our brands, let us at least do it with porous walls and wide and generous gates of entry.

A New Thought Liberation Theology constructed as such would make ample room for new voices, an array of contributors, and diverse expressions. Holmes understood this principle when he sought out Rev. "Mother" Pearl C. Wood in East Los Angeles. He listened intently to her teaching and instantly recognized the common thread. He invited her to join the Religious Science movement, not at the cost of her other affiliations but with the inclusion of them.

While New Thought always has included a collection of diverse voices, it must be deliberate in its inclusion of voices that don't fit the expected norm of spiritual voices. Let's include the likes of Bishop John Shelby Spong, Bishop Carlton D. Pearson, D.E. Paulk, and Bishop Dr. Yvette Flunder. Let's also incorporate the deep wisdom of James Baldwin, Alice Walker, bell hooks, Toni Morrison, Maya Angelou, and Angela Davis, to name just a few.

PARTICULAR AND UNIVERSAL

One of the things a New Thought Liberation Movement will need to come to terms with is the power of the particular within the universal. Historically, the movement tended to focus on the universal within the particular. While each perspective has its value, a movement of inclusion and oneness demands a both/and approach.

At one end of this perspective is the universal within the particular. This is the level called "Universal Truths," which can be seen across diverse spaces and places. It is where we can gain wisdom from archetypes whose characteristics cross boundaries of culture and context. This is the hero's journey. The concept of the archetype explains why we can see ourselves or each other in movies or across a wide spectrum of human history and say, "I know that person," or "I am just like that"

Much of New Thought literature and teaching exists at this level. It seeks to extract a universal wisdom from the ages and boil it down to its essence. And much of our teaching and writings are from teachers with a seemingly gifted ability to extract the universal truth from various particular sources: Emma Curtis Hopkins, Ralph Waldo Emerson, Thomas Troward, H. Emilie Cady, Charles Filmore, Ernest Holmes. Yet a New Thought Liberation Theology must remain free (liberated) from its own sacred cows, the temptation to overly venerate its founders into a space too far beyond where power and privilege already placed them.

Let me be clear: Finding the universal from the particular is a perfectly acceptable way of discovering and learning about ourselves, about spirituality, and about the tools of consciousness. However, the danger here is that it becomes too tempting to think only via the universal, believing there is simple and generic wisdom in the atmosphere, nameless and up for grabs. This comes uncomfortably close to a colonizing mindset, as established in the doctrine discovery. While we may have every reason to believe that Phineas Parkhurt Quimby and others came by their insights honestly, we also know that Thomas Troward spent a considerable amount of his adult life in India, surrounded by Hindu wisdom, which is pronounced and without credit in his writings. Ernest Holmes was called the great synthesizer, and there is no doubting his mental capacity to see the universal wisdom running through many streams. Yet we can—and must—also hold him accountable for not crediting the sources of his wisdom. This is not just a product of their time, an era in which footnote sourcing was less of a standard, as much of the same can be said for the work of people like Wayne Dyer and others today. Yes, the One Mind contains all knowledge, but so does the library.

At the other end is the particular within the universal. At this level, we see that within the universal story or an individual archetype is a particular nuance, specificity, and uniqueness that does not take away from the universal element or characteristic. While we are all the same (universal), we are also all unique and different. Similarly, the universal wisdom we attempt to lay claim to must be applied at the practical level and particular context of humanity. That particular context also contains wisdom, relevance, and insight. As such, it will inform the unfolding of spiritual experience just as much as the universal wisdom.

Too often we dismiss the particular, naming it as mere condition and secondary. Doing so leads to the dismissal of cultural context, wisdom, and contributions that cannot be seen or experienced in any other way other than in the particular. In her book, *Stained Glass Spirit: Becoming a Spiritual Community Where Oneness Does Not Require Sameness,* Dr. Tracy Brown, RScP, is correct when she asserts, "Oneness does not mean sameness." Just because we share a universal aspect of our being does not mean our unique views and experiences are less valuable, significant, or informative to our personal and collective unfolding.

> *The career of Jesus shows that his work
> was directed to the oppressed for the purpose
> of their liberation. To suggest that he was speaking
> of a "spiritual" liberation fails to take seriously Jesus's thoroughly
> Hebrew view of human nature.*
>
> — James H. Cone, A Black Theology of Liberation,
> Fortieth Anniversary Edition

Similarly, for New Thought to insist in any form that the liberation it promotes is simply "spiritual liberation"—i.e. generic or universal in nature and thus left to each individual to work out what that means—fails to take seriously the contextual reality and particularity within the universal stories of liberation throughout religious history. The particular circumstances of Jesus of Nazerith, Siddhartha Gautama, Arjuna, Moses, and Mohamed each provide critical insights and clues into the essence of spiritual liberation and universal truth.

CONCLUSION

As I mentioned in the opening pages of this book, my journey into a more practical and relevant 21st century version of New Thought was launched by the works of Shariff Abdullah in his book *Creating A World that Works for All*. As I bring this to a close, I return to these familiar pages. He reminds us that being "an activist for an inclusive society is a spiritual discipline. ... Working to alleviate suffering is the way we practice our faith." He further lays out the measure of success by which we can integrate New Thought's long-standing focus on personal development and its newfound vision for a world that works for all. He writes: "Success doesn't mean I've saved an endangered species or cleaned up a toxic waste dump or fed hungry children. Success means awakening in myself a Spirit that can help make a better life for others. Success means I have acted in the world as though I were part of it, not apart from it. Success means becoming conscious of and faithful to my values and to my soul."

A New Thought Liberation Theology seeks to unite head and heart. It makes room for the activist and the mystic, the marching and the meditating, the affirming and the calling out. It seeks to make community and gathering as important as personal time and introspection. It seeks to elevate both action and contemplation as means of demonstration.

For New Thought to be relevant, it must make this journey from the head to the heart. It must learn to put a name to its universal love of humanity and get specific about what a world that works for everyone means to the individual, in real and stark and tangible terms.

Once New Thought gets clear about this, it must then ask itself if it is serious about making it real. While there is no doubt in my mind that the debate about how to go about this will continue, it is my prayer that the movement does not die on the sword of righteousness in the process. Let us make room for diverse expressions without the need to take down another. Let our embrace of liberation as a principle live in liberation as a practice. Let us release it in expressions known and unknown, tried and untried, innovative and traditional. I believe the future of liberation teaching lives in a contextual reality. What works in one area may not work elsewhere, and vice versa. Yet all should be received as authentic attempts to set free by the laws of consciousness those we have particular access to.

Moreover, let us seek to demonstrate the truth that we hold dear, knowing and remembering that demonstration is the only authority. ∞

1. In this chapter, we explore the "Kingdoms/Realms of Consciousness" model. Have you heard of this model, and, if so, have you used it in your spiritual growth work?

_____

_____

_____

_____

_____

_____

2. What is your reaction to the addition of a Fifth Realm, AS WE, to the model? Do you see this as a necessary addition?

_____

_____

_____

_____

_____

_____

3. Chapter Seven summarizes the work in the previous chapters. Do you think the author made a compelling case for New Thought as a liberation theology? What stood out to you the most about making this case?

_____

_____

_____

_____

_____

_____

4. What is next? If, as the author states, this work is just the beginning of a new chapter in the history of New Thought and expanded consciousness, what do you think comes next? Where does it go from here?

_____

_____

_____

_____

_____

_____

TWELVE PRINCIPLES OF RADICAL INCLUSIVITY

Note from Rev. Dr. David Alexander: One of the voices that must be included in a New Thought Liberation Theology is that of Bishop Dr. Yvette Flunder, whose personal and theological journey of liberation exemplifies the principles of personal responsibility and collective activism. I am humbled and grateful to have had her friendship, mentorship, and support in my ministerial journey over the years.

TWELVE PRINCIPLES OF RADICAL INCLUSIVITY: A MODEL FOR RECOVERY FROM OPPRESSIVE AND EXCLUSIVE THEOLOGIES AND RELIGIONS

I am a third-generation pastor and bishop, baptized in the realities of religion both at its best and worse—religion as a liberator and as a violator of human rights. I embody this reality in my trifecta persona as an African American, same-gender-loving woman, and clergy person. I have been raised in and put out by the church. The church has infected my soul with a love of people, gospel music, spirit-filled worship, and miracle-working power. The same church has also rejected me for who I am, for who I love, and for the call on my life to serve the church.

These are the beautiful and painful realities that coexist in me. I am living proof that liberation and emancipation are necessary and possible.

Religion has done beautiful work to serve humanity, while simultaneously being a principle harbinger of oppression and exclusion in the lives of women, people of color, and the LGBTQIA+ community. Religious addiction and power over dynamics at the expense of others' needs a twelve-step recovery program, a healing. The church needs liberation from what we have done to it.

The holy work of inclusivity can no longer be passive. No more closet prophets. Come out, come out, wherever you are! People's lives depend on our yes. My brother, David Alexander, is one such prophet who has come out to stand boldly in the public square, shoulder to shoulder with his siblings on the margins. He's not afraid, because he knows his own destiny and freedom are tied up in mine.

The future of religion must be built on the principles of radical inclusivity and shouldered by broad coalitions of prophets and torchbearers from diverse streams and backgrounds.

An inclusive movement is and must be radical. Inclusivity, with love for all of God's creation, challenges major fundamental, deep-seated beliefs, doctrines, and theologies at the center of our society. These beliefs often characterize people who do not fit the definition of an acceptable social norm as enemies of God and routinely mistreats, oppresses, and excludes people from the community of faith and its institutions.

A radical and inclusive movement recognizes, values, loves, and celebrates people on the margins of society. Jesus himself was from the edge of society, and his was a ministry to those who were considered "least." Jesus's public ministry and associations were primarily with the poor, weak, outcasts, foreigners, and prostitutes.

A radically inclusive movement must recognize harm done in the name of God. Many people rejected by religion got their "church burns" from Bible-believing Christian flamethrowers. Contempt for the church and all things religious often stems from exposure to oppressive theology, self-serving biblical literalism, and unyielding tradition. It is neither Christlike nor spiritual to be oppressive. No human being is born with a destiny to be oppressed or to oppress others.

A radically inclusive movement is intentional and creates ministry on the margins on purpose—because of the radically inclusive love of God. The inclusive community deliberately makes a conscious and unapologetic decision to love and celebrate the Creator's diversity. Welcoming all persons regardless of race, color, ancestry, age, gender, and sexual or affectional orientation. Radical inclusivity practices and celebrates the Christian community outside of the dominant culture, believing that the kingdom (kin-dom) of God includes the margins of society and is a perfect place for ministry. Marginalized people, now as in the time of Jesus's Earthly ministry, respond to a community of openness and extravagant grace, where other people from the edge gather. Such an atmosphere welcomes people, enabling them to feel it is safe to be who they are.

The primary goal of a radically inclusive movement is not to imitate or change the mainline church, but rather to be church. The church belongs to God and is the Body of Jesus Christ. It is not the sole property of any denomination, person, or group. There are systemic wrongs in organized religion due to oppressive theology, bibliolatry, and traditional beliefs, which prevent freedom for all people, that we can never fully set right. Radical inclusivity, however, is ministry rooted in restoration, based on believing that God has given us the work and ministry of reconciliation. "It is for freedom that Christ has set us free" (Galatians 5:1). Although radical inclusivity believes in and celebrates the kinship and fellowship of all, it does not seek to change mainline religion. Instead, it uses its power of love to model and demonstrate the radically inclusive love of Jesus Christ.

A radically inclusive movement requires a new way of seeing and a new way of being. "From now on, therefore, we regard no one from a human point of view; even though we once knew Christ from a human point of view, we know him no longer in that way" (2 Corinthians 5:16). This scripture passage implies that we can celebrate one another in some new and powerful way in community, some way that both accepts who each of us is in a human sense and transcends our humanity, allowing us to see each other as God sees us. Faith-filled community can truly be celebrated when we realize the church is a spiritual, mystical, faith community, and we relate best when we make the two-foot drop from head to heart.

A radically inclusive movement requires awareness, information, and understanding. The creation of faith-based community among people marginalized by religion requires that the community be prepared and maintain a presence of cultural familiarity through education and training that equips the community to understand, actively fight, and overcome oppressive and exclusive theology and practices. Sustaining and eventually celebrating community on the margin requires the church to reexamine sexual and relational ethics, develop a theology of welcome, and destigmatize views of any group of people.

A radically inclusive movement does not hide, and it works to undo shame and fear. The radically inclusive ministry of Jesus does not encourage people to hide their unacceptable realities (based on the dominant culture's point of view or faith) in order to be embraced. True community comes when marginalized people take back the right to fully be. People must celebrate, not in spite of who they are, but because of who their Creator made them to be. For marginalized people to have community, they must develop community, naked with their marginality in full view, while often celebrating the very thing that separates them from the dominant culture.

Radically inclusive movements must recognize diversity on the margins. People live and are located on the various margins of society for many reasons. Most people live on the margin because dominant cultures and/or faith communities force them outside their boundaries to a margin. Not all marginalized people are poor, uneducated, or visible. Because many marginalized people are together on the margin does not mean each affirms the other or that their common marginality will hold the community together. People on the margins are challenged to find the inter-connectedness and the intersections of their marginalities.

Radical inclusivity must be linked to preaching and teaching. The creation of Christian community among people marginalized by the church requires preaching and teaching that defines and strengthens the essence of the community through a theology of radical inclusivity. Preaching and teaching clarifies, reinforces, and supports the collective theology of the community, giving voice to its emergence and evolution.

Radical inclusivity demands hospitality. Marginalized people experience hospitality where they do not have to defend or deny their place or their humanness. Hospitality means primarily the creation of a free space where the stranger can enter and become a friend instead of an enemy. Hospitality is not a means to change people, but instead offers them space where change can take place. It does not bring men and women over to "our side," but instead offers the freedom to not disturbed by a dividing line. It does not lead our neighbor into a corner where there are no alternatives left, but instead opens a wide spectrum of options for choice and commitment. It is not a method of making our God and our way into the criteria of happiness, but the opening of an opportunity to others to find their God and their way. Hospitality is not a subtle invitation to adopt the lifestyle of the host, but the gift of chance for the guest to find their own.

A radically inclusive movement is best sustained and celebrated when everyone in the community is responsible and accountable. Sustaining faith-based community requires an intentional effort to design a framework that includes everyone. The dissemination of duties and chores ensures that all members share in and contribute to the welfare of the community. It is often difficult for people who have not had continuity in life to understand that freedom without responsibility and accountability is as detrimental as slavery. Freedom cannot be an end unto itself. Freedom from something must flow into freedom to be something else, or it is not truly freedom.

The object of getting free is being free. The object of being free is living free. Here's to a freedom and liberation attained by all. ∞

– Bishop Yvette A. Flunder,
City of Refuge UCC, Oakland, California
Founder and Presiding Bishop,
The Fellowship of Affirming Ministries

PROPHETIC JUSTICE PRINCIPLES FROM REV. DR. JAMES FORBES

Undoubtably the next leg of our journey together will continue to evolve, as will the principles of a meta-spiritual justice movement. My sincere prayer is that this book marks just the beginning of many contributions from diverse voices on the subject of New Thought Liberation Theology.

To begin that contribution, I want include here a few inspirational voices and works I believe can help shape where we go from here.

In his lecture series, "Prophetic Justice Principles," Rev. Dr. James Forbes, of Riverside Church in New York City, offers guidance for following "prophetic justice principles," by which people of faith should test their leaders' policies:

1. Seek the common good: Does the policy represent the common good rather than the interests of an elite few?

2. Be truthful in facts and motives: Is the policy based on a true analysis and does it disclose its true intention? How likely is the policy to achieve its proposed purpose?

3. Promote unity and inclusion: Does the policy hold the prospect of reducing the polarization and fragmentation of society due to race, religion, class, gender, sexual orientation, or national origin?

4. Care for the poor: Does the policy provide good news for the poor? Does it reverse the trend toward an ever-widening gap between rich and poor?

5. Protect the vulnerable: Is the policy good for the children, the elderly, and the disadvantaged? Does it show sensitivity to the spirit of the Golden Rule?

6. Guard freedom of thought and discussion: Does the policy provide for free press, free discussion, and the expression of dissent, along with fair and just methods of participation in the democratic process?

7. Respect other nations and peoples: Does the policy encourage respect for peoples and nations other than our own? Does it respect the fundamental dignity of every human being? Does it use diplomacy as a valued instrument of statecraft in resolving international conflicts and refrain from unilateral military actions for empire-building and domination strategies?

8. Ensure stewardship of creation: Is the policy supportive of strong measures to ensure ecological responsibility and sustainability?

9. Cherish the human family: Does the policy practice good global citizenship, involving respect for all cultures and nations, and collective responsibility for the common good of the global community? Does it refrain from nationalism, militarism, or imperialism based on a sense of national superiority?

10. Provide moral leadership: Does the policy lead by example, doing the right thing and holding the right lessons for our children and our citizens? Does it promote a more ethical society, and uphold trust in public offices? ∞

ERNEST HOLMES, "SERMON BY THE SEA"

Presented on Saturday, August 15, 1959

Our religion is not something to be lived merely here at Asilomar, as much inspiration as we receive from it, but rather to take that consciousness we have arrived at here back with us into whatever activities we may be engaged in. I do not believe life is separated from its living, anywhere.

There is nothing in the world that can take the place of love, friendship, appreciation, and cooperation in our lives. I have thought so much about this all week, because these are the only things that have any meaning in the eternal values in which we are so interested. Emerson said that it is very easy for us to maintain a spiritual equilibrium in solitude, "but the great man is he who in the midst of the crowd keeps with perfect sweetness the independence of solitude."

I do not believe there is a single fact in human history or a single manifestation in the universe that is or could possibly be anything other than a manifestation of the One Divine Mind, the One Universal Presence, the One Infinite Spirit.

It seems to me that it is only as we view all life, everything from what we call great to what we call small, important or unimportant, it is only as we view the whole thing, as Alexander Pope, who said, "one stupendous whole, whose body nature is and God the soul," that we shall really enter into communion, into sympathetic oneness and rapport with the reality of all that is about us. Someone asked me, "What do you think God is?" I looked out the window and said, "I think God is that tree." And there was a squirrel running up the tree, and I said, "I think God is that squirrel."

It is going to be absolutely impossible for us, with our finite comprehension, to have the intelligence to divide the indivisible and to say this is real and that is unreal. The marketplace is as real as is the temple. That is why Jesus said that it is neither in the temple at Jerusalem nor in the mountain but in yourself that the secret of life is discovered, that the soul of the universe is consciously entered into, and the divine and benign Spirit, which indwells everything, is loosed in Its splendor and power through you, through your partnership with the Infinite, through your oneness with God, the living Spirit.

Everything that lives proclaims the glory of God. Every person who exists manifests the life of God. There is one Spirit in which we live, one Mind by which we think, one body of which we are a part, and one light that lighteth every man's pathway.

We are a part of the evolution of human destiny. We are a part of the unfoldment of the divine intelligence in human affairs. It has reached the point of conscious and deliberate cooperation with that principle of evolution and out-push of the creative urge of the Spirit, on this planet at least, to bring about innumerable centers that It may enjoy. Also we may enjoy it through that divine interior awareness, which is the intercommunication of God with man, revealing our own divine nature.

Having had the privilege of starting Religious Science, I would wish, will, and desire above all things else that the simplicity and purity of our teaching could never be violated. There is a purpose of simplicity, a consciousness of unity, a straight-line thinking in our philosophy that has never appeared before in the world, outside of the teachings of men like Jesus and Emerson.

There was nothing obscure in the teaching of Jesus. He just said that is "the Father's good pleasure to give you the kingdom." Why don't you take it? He said that there is nothing but God. Why don't believe it? He was the last of the great Jewish prophets, the greatest line of emotional prophets the world has ever known.

The Greeks had the greatest intellectual perception of the ages. It appears in their literature and art, a perfect thing without a soul.

We also find a great intellectualism in Emerson, who never contradicted himself. He gave us the simplest statement of intellectual spiritual perception, probably that has ever been put into print. As that of Jesus, it was simplest, most direct, meaningful and full of feeling. We inherit this.

It would be my desire that simplicity and purity and directness, that straight thinking should never depart from the teachings of our practitioners or instructions of our teachers or understanding of our laymen. It is the most direct impartation of divine wisdom that has ever come to the world because it incorporates the precepts of Jesus and Emerson and Buddha and all the rest of the wise. And I would desire that in our teaching, there would never be any arrogance, for it always indicates spiritual immaturity to me. Others will arise who will know more than we do. They won't be better or worse. They will be different and know more than we do. Evolution is forward.

I would desire that we should not build, out of the body of our simplicity and grandeur and beauty, other creeds loaded with superstition, a fear of the unknown, and a dread of the unseen. We have discovered a "pearl of great price." We have discovered the rarest gem that has ever found, setting in the intellect of the human race complete simplicity, complete directness, a freedom from fear and superstition about the unknown and about God.

And we have rediscovered that which the great, the good, and the wise have sung about and thought about: the imprisoned splendor within ourselves and within each other, and we have direct contact with it. Whether we call it the Christ in us or the Buddha or Atman or just the Son of God the living Spirit, makes no difference. You and I are witness to the divine fact, and we have discovered an authority beyond our minds, even though our minds utilize it. Out of this, we have prepared ourselves, I think, I hope, I pray and believe.

One cannot but feel, from the human point in such meetings as these, that it is entirely possible one might not be here next year. This is of complete indifference to me because I believe in life, and I feel fine. Such an event is merely the climax of human events in anybody's life, and it is to be looked forward to, not with dread or fear or apprehension but as the next great adventure, and one that we should all be very happy and glad to experience.

But we must weigh and measure things somewhat from the human angle. No person or organization can make the provision for that which is paramount, for that which is of the most stupendous importance, that out of the ranks of all of us, innumerable people shall grow up who shall have caught a vision, who shall have seen a glory, who shall have experienced God.

The thing that interests me now is that every man shall find his savior within himself. If this is the only place he is going to discover God, you may be sure it is the only avenue through which any way-shower shall lead him to God. There is no other way. Jesus knew this, and when they sought to make Jesus, the man, the way, he said that it was expedient he go away that the spirit of truth should awaken within his followers the knowledge and understanding of what he had been talking about, that he had come to reveal them to themselves.

As we think, speak, talk, and commune with each other and with nature and God, there will never be an answer to us beyond the level of our approach. The level of our approach is the only avenue through which there could be an answer, else we would not be individuals. God cannot make a mechanical spontaneity, and that is why we are left alone to discover ourselves.

Those who bear witness in consciousness do not need to retire from life. The great man is he who, in the midst of the crowd, can keep with perfect simplicity the independence of his solitude. It is not in the mountain or the temple in Jerusalem. It is in our own heart, our own mind, our own consciousness, our own being, where we live twenty-four hours a day, awake or asleep, that the eternal share of the Infinite comes to us, because every man is some part of the essence of God, not as a fragment, yet as totality.

I think we have brought a blessing to the world, the possibility of something expressing through us that has never before been given to the world—a simplicity, a sincerity, and, I trust, a love and understanding. But we too little practice it because the human mind is prone, even when it has discovered a greater good than it had before, to compare the degree of good it thinks it possesses with a lesser degree of good it thinks someone else has. And this is brought about only through the psychological projection of some unredeemed past of a person's own psyche.

You will never discover a person who is full of emotional judgment and condemnation of others who is doing anything other than unconsciously releasing the tension of a burden, a burden so great to be born that he does not even permit it to come to the light of day to be seen, for he could not face it. This has been scientifically proved. And that is why Jesus, with the profoundness of utmost simplicity, did not say, judge not lest God will judge you. He knew better. He said, "Judge not, that ye be not judged. For with what judgment ye judge, ye shall be judged." In other words, your judgment will judge you. "And with what measure ye mete, it will be measured to you again." God is not going to measure it back to you and say, I will show you who is boss. You are the measure-outer. Troward said that we are dispensers of the divine gift and we are in partnership with the Infinite.

It would be wonderful indeed if a group of persons should arrive on Earth who were for something and against nothing. This would be the *summum bonum* (Latin for the highest good) of human organization, wouldn't it? It is in the life of the individual.

Find me one person who is for something and against nothing, who is redeemed enough not to condemn others out of the burden of his soul, and I will find another savior, another Jesus and an exalted human being.

Find me one person who no longer has any fear of the universe or of God or of man or of anything else, and you will have brought to me someone in whose presence we may sit, and fear shall vanish as clouds before the sunlight.

Find me someone who has redeemed his own soul, and he shall become my redeemer.

Find me someone who has given all that he has in love, without morbidity, and I will have found the lover of my soul. Is not this true? Why? Because he will have revealed to me the nature of God and proved to me the possibility of all human souls.

This is what Religious Science stands for. It is not a new dogmatism. It is not a new authority generated from a new alleged revelation of the God who never revealed anything to anybody, as such, else He could not have revealed all things to all people. There is no special dispensation of Providence, but there is a specialized dispensation that the great and good and wise and just have known, even though they knew it intuitively.

Find me one person who can get his own littleness out of the way, and he shall reveal to me the immeasurable magnitude of the universe in which I live.

Find me one person who knows how to talk to God, really, and I shall walk with him through the woods, and everything that seems inanimate will respond. The leaves of the trees will clap their hands; the grass will grow soft under him.

Find me one person who communes with cause and effect, and in the evening, the evening star will sing to him and the darkness will turn to light. Through him, as the woman who touched the hem of the garment of Christ was healed, shall I be healed of all loneliness forever.

Find me someone who is no longer sad, whose memory has been redeemed from morbidity, and I shall hear laughter.

Find me someone whose song is really celestial because it is the outburst of the cosmic urge to sing, and I shall hear the music of the spheres.

"All things are delivered unto me of my Father, and no man knoweth the Son but the Father. Neither knoweth any man the Father, save the Son and he to whomsoever the Son will reveal Him." And each of us is that son. No use waiting for avatars. Jesus is not coming again; he is wiser than that. He has earned whatever he has. And to you and to me, no single kernel of grain shall come unless we have planted it. No meal shall be made unless we have ground it, no bread baked unless we have kneaded it and put it in the oven of our own consciousness, where the silent processes of an invisible and ineffable light precipitates itself into that which for us stands for the start of life.

But how we have put off that day! We say to each other that we don't know enough, we aren't good enough. The ignorance of our unknowing, the blindness of our unseeing, the condemnation of the ages weighing against our consciousness, known and unknown, conscious and unconscious, has created the greatest possibility of the larger progress of humanity, a burden so tremendous that even men's adoration of God has been saddened by fear. Like the man Ernest Renan said, prayed, "O God, if there be a God, save my soul if I have a soul." He did not know, so he was afraid to take a chance.

Find me one person who no longer doubts, no longer waivers, but not one who, with a proclamation of superiority, says, "Look at me. I have arrived!" I will not listen to that. Only that which reveals me to myself can be a message to me. Only that which gives me back myself can save me. Only that which leads me to the God within myself can reveal God. And only that person can do it to whom the vision has come through his own efforts, through the gift of God. Of course, the grace of God abounds by divine givingness. God has forever hung Himself upon the cross of men's indifference. God has forever, but without suffering, given Himself, but we have not received the gift.

Find me one person who has so completely divorced from himself all arrogance, and you will have discovered for me an open pathway to the kingdom of God, here and now. Up until now, the search has been in far-off corners of the Earth. And we have knelt upon a prayer rug and been wafted away, in our morbid and fearful imagination, over ethers of nothingness, to places that have no existence—the temples of our unbelief—and we have come back empty. "What went ye out into the wilderness for to see?"

And now comes Religious Science. We are no more sincere than others. If we felt we were, that would be a projection of our insincerity. We are no better. If we thought we were, that would be a projection of an unconscious sense of guilt. Anyway, it would be stupid, and there is no greater sin on Earth than just plain stupidity.

What shall reveal the self to the self? The self shall raise the self by the self.

Find me somebody who has detached his emotional and psycholog-ical ego from the real self, without having to deny the place it plays in the scheme of things and without slaying any part of himself because the transcendence is there also, and I will have discovered the Ineffable in this individual and a direct pathway for the communion of my own soul.

Now, what does this all mean? I am talking about you and about my-self. When I say, "Find a person," I don't mean to go over to Rome or London or back to your own church. The search is not external. All of these people I have been talking about have no existence as such, other than as figments of my own imagination, until they are finally centered in our own soul. Then this guest for whom we are looking will be the Self redeemed from the lesser self. This is a very interesting thing, for nature is foolproof, and when the fruit is ripe it will fall. When the kingdom of

God is perceived, it will be experienced simultaneously, instantaneously, and in its entirety.

But these people all exist in us. They are different attributes, qualities of our own soul. They are different visions, not that we have multiple or dual personalities, but that every one of us on that inner side of life is, has been, and shall remain in eternal communion with the Ineffable, where he may know that he is no longer with God, but one of God. If it were not for that which echoes eternally down the corridors of our own minds, some voice that ever sings in our own souls, some urge that continuously presses us forward, there would be no advance in our science or religion or in the humanities or anything else. But "He left not himself without witness."

These are simple things that call for discipline, not as one normally thinks of discipline, but a different kind of discipline that one discovers. I often sit for several hours at a time, sometimes all day, thinking one simple thought. No matter what it is, it isn't a waste of time to find out what this thought means to me or what it should mean in my life or what it would mean everywhere. This is something no one can do for us but ourselves. We are "the way, the truth and the life."

We have come to Asilomar, spent this wonderful week together on love for each other and adoration for the God we believe in. Many wonderful things have happened that would seem miracles if we didn't know about them. And now we meet for this fond farewell after the spiritual bath of peace, the baptism of the spirit. Not through me but you to me and I to you, through each other, the revelation of the self to the self. We go back into the highways and byways of life with something so great that never again will anything be quite the same. A little more light shall come, a little greater glory added to the glory we already possess, a deeper consciousness, a higher aspiration, a broader certainty of the mind.

You are Religious Science. I am not. I am only the one who put something together. I do not even take myself seriously, but I take what I am doing seriously. You are Religious Science: our ministers, our teachers, our practitioners, our laymen. You find me 1,000 people in the world who know what Religious Science is and use it and live it as it is, and I'll myself live to see a new world, a new heaven, and a new Earth here. There is a cosmic Power wrapped up in a cosmic consciousness and purposiveness that is equal to the vision which looses It.

What I am saying is this: There is a law that backs up the vision, and the law is immutable. "Heaven and Earth shall pass away, but my words shall not pass away." There is a power transcendent beyond our needs, our little wants. Demonstrating a dime is good if one needs it, or healing oneself of a pain is certainly good if one has it, but beyond that, at the real feast at the tabernacle of the Almighty, in the temple of the living God, in the banquet hall of heaven, there is something beyond anything that you and I have touched.

Find 1,000 people who know that and use it, and the world will no longer be famished. How important it is that each one of us in his simple way shall live from God to God, with God, in God, and to each other. That is why we are here. And we are taking back with us, I trust, a vision and an inspiration, something beyond a hope and a longing, that the living Spirit shall through us walk anew into Its own creation and a new glory come with a new dawn.

"Now the Lord is in His holy temple, et all the earth keep silent before Him, as we drink deeply from the perennial fountain of eternal life, as we partake of the bread of heaven, and as we open wide the gates of our consciousness that the King of Glory shall come in.

And may God bless and keep us. And for all the love you have given me, may I bless you. ∞

CENTERS FOR SPIRITUAL LIVING VISION STATEMENT

We envision all people, all beings, and all life as expressions of God.

We see a world in which each and every person lives in alignment with their highest spiritual principle, emphasizing unity with God and connection with each other; a world in which individually and collectively we are called to a higher state of consciousness and action.

We envision humanity awakening to its spiritual magnificence and discovering the creative power of thought; a world where each and every person discovers their own personal power and ability to create an individual life that works within a world that works for everyone.

We envision a world in which we live and grow as One Global Family that respects and honors the interconnectedness of all life; a world where this kinship with all life prospers and connects through the guidance of spiritual wisdom and experience.

We envision a world where personal responsibility joins with social conscience in every area of the political, corporate, academic, and social sectors, providing sustainable structures to further the emerging global consciousness.

We envision a world where each and every person has enough food, a home and a sense of belonging; a world of peace and harmony, enfranchisement and justice.

We envision a world in which resources are valued, cared for, and grown, and where there is generous and continuous sharing of these resources.

We envision a worldwide culture in which forgiveness (whether for errors, injustices, or debts) is the norm.

We envision a world which has renewed its emphasis on beauty, nature, and love through the resurgence of creativity, art, and aesthetics.

We envision a world that works for everyone and for all of creation.

UNITY'S STATEMENT OF SOCIAL ACTION POSITION

Webster defines the word "unity" as "the state of forming a complete and pleasing whole... ." At this time in the evolution of the planet and the lives of human beings upon it, the task of "forming a complete and pleasing whole" is the imperative for positive evolution and harmonious existence for all.

This perspective has seemingly been lost—our wholeness, our oneness, our sameness as a human race. We must now remember more than ever, that we have much more in common than that which divides us.

The Unity movement stands for and will tirelessly work for harmony so all people may know the freedom of peaceful expression; so they may know their own inner worth and essential contribution to the whole of life.

- Where there are divisions of opinions, beliefs, and perspectives, Unity embraces curiosity, exploration, and expanded awareness of the gifts of diversity.

- Where there is fear of "the other," Unity stands for inclusivity and peaceful acceptance of another's right to create the life of his or her choosing.

- Where there is oppression and hatred, we stand for justice and understanding, and for extending compassion, kindness, and forgiveness to restore balance.

- Where there is discrimination, we stand for inclusivity and equality. We pledge to be an advocate for the well-being, respect, and civil freedom of every human being.

Any proposal or action that seeks to discriminate against individuals or classes of individuals based on prejudiced, stereotypic profiles of national origin, class, creed, race, ethnicity, physical ability, sexual orientation, or gender identity is in opposition to the core beliefs and values established by our founders.

We choose Unity. In harmony with the divine Spirit we stand, so we may live in a spiritually awakened world that is continually evolving.

This is our prayer and our decree. Through our actions, we let it be.

REFERENCES

Abdullah, Sharif. *Creating a World that Works for All*. San Francisco: Berrett-Koehler Publishers, 1999.

Armstrong, Karen. *Fields of Blood: Religion and the History of Violence*. New York: Anchor Books, 2015.

Atkinson, William Walker and Rev. Lux Newman & Quimby Society. *The Law Of The New Thought: A Study Of Fundamental Principles & Their Application*. Chicago: The Psychic Research Company, 1902.

Bailies, Gil. *Violence Unveiled: Humanity at the Crossroads*. New York: The Crossroad Publishing Company, 2017.

Beckwith, Michael Bernard. *Life Visioning: A Transformative Process for Activating Your Unique Gifts and Highest Potential*. Boulder, Colorado: Sounds True, 2012.

Bennett, Arnold. *My Religion*. London: Hutchinson & Co., 1925.

Borg, Marcus J. *Convictions: A manifesto for progressive Christians*. London: Ashford Colour Press, 2014.

Brown, Tracy. *Stained Glass Spirit: Becoming a Spiritual Community Where Oneness Does Not Require Sameness*. Self-published, 2019.

Brueggemann, Walter. *The Prophetic Imagination*. Philadelphia: Fortress Press, 1978.

Campbell, Joseph. *The Power of Myth*. New York: Anchor Books, 1991.

Charles, Mark and Soong-Chan Rah. *Unsettling Truths: The Ongoing, Dehumanizing Legacy of the Doctrine of Discovery*. Downers Grove, Illinois: InterVarsity Press, 2019.

Cone, James. *A Black Theology of Liberation. 50th Anniversary Edition*. Ossining, New York: Orbis Books, 2020.

Cone, James. *For My People: Black Theology and the Black Church*. Maryknoll, New York: Orbis Books, 1984.

Cone, James. *Black Theology, Black Power*. Maryknoll, New York: Orbis Books, 1997 and 2019.

Dethmer, Jim, Diana Chapman, and Kaley Klemp. *The 15 Commitments of Conscious Leadership: A New Paradigm for Sustainable Success.* Self-published, 2014.

Dresser, Horatio Willis, Phineas Parkhurst Quimby, Mary Baker Eddy, Warren Felt Evans, Thomas Troward, et al. *A History of the New Thought Movement.* Publisher unknown, 1919.

Fillmore, Myrtle. *Healing Letters.* WestPub Online, 2015.

———. *How to Let God Help You.* WestPub Online, 2015.

Fuller, Margaret. *Woman in the Nineteenth Century.* Mineola, New York: Dover Publications, 1999.

Girard, René. *Violence and the Sacred.* English Translation 1977. Baltimore: The Johns Hopkins University Press, 1972.

Grant, Jacquelyn. *White Women's Christ and Black Women's Jesus: Feminist Christology and Womanist Response.* Atlanta: Scholars Press, 1989.

Haller, John S. *The History of New Thought: From Mind Cure to Positive Thinking and the Prosperity Gospel.* West Chester, Pennsylvania: Swedenborg Foundation Press, 2012.

Holmes, Fenwicke, and Masaharu Taniguchi. *The Science of Faith: How To Make Yourself Believe.* Publisher unknown, 1962.

McLaren, Brian D. *Everything Must Change:When the World's Biggest Problems and Jesus' Good News Collide.* Nashville: Thomas Nelson, Inc., 2007.

Myerson, Joel, ed. *A Historical Guide to Ralph Waldo Emerson (Historical Guides to American Authors).* Oxford: Oxford University Press, 2000.

Nepo, Mark. *More Together Than Alone: Discovering the Power and Spirit of Community in Our Lives and in the World.* New York: Atria, 2018.

Pontiac, Ronnie. *American Metaphysical Religion: Esoteric and Mystical Traditions of the New World.* Rochester, Vermont: Inner Traditions, 2023.

Putman, Robert. *Bowling Alone: The Collapse and Revival of American Community.* New York: Simon and Schuster, 2020.

Quart, Alissa. *Bootstrapped: Liberating Ourselves from the American Dream.* New York: HarperCollins Publishers, 2023.

Riley, Cole Arthur. *Black Liturgies: Poems, Prayers, and Meditations for Staying Human.* New York: Convergent Books, 2024.

Satter, Beryl. *Each Mind a Kingdom: American Women, Sexual Purity, and the New Thought Movement, 1875-1920.* Berkeley and Los Angeles, California: University of California Press, 1999.

Scott, Josh. *Bible Stories for Grown Ups: Reading Scripture with New Eyes.* Nashville: Abington Press, 2023.

Tocqueville, Alexis de. *Democracy in America and Two Essays on America.* London: Penguin Group, 2003.

Turner, Jack. *Awakening to Race: Individualism and Social Consciousness in America.* Chicago: University of Chicago Press, 2012.

Washington, Joseph R. *Black Religion: The Negro and Christianity in the United States.* Lanham, Maryland: University Press of America, 1984.

ABOUT THE AUTHOR

Rev. David Alexander, DD, became a licensed Religious Science practitioner in 1999 and graduated with honors from the University of New Mexico in 2000. In 2004, he cofounded the New Thought Center for Spiritual Living and served as its senior minister for 15 years. In 2014, he received an honorary Doctor of Divinity degree from Centers for Spiritual Living. He currently serves as spiritual director of the Spiritual Living Center of Atlanta.

A social justice activist, he has served on numerous community boards, including eleven years on the board of directors for the Community of Welcoming Congregations, a Portland-based alliance with the mission of "providing a voice for LGBTQIA+ and allied people of faith." He served for eight years on the Leadership Council for Centers for Spiritual Living, including two terms as chair, and in 2021 on the Diversity, Equity, Race Commission for the City of Brookhaven, Georgia, as well as the Leadership Council for the Association for Global New Thought.

He was inducted into the Martin Luther King Jr. Board of Preachers at Morehouse College in 2009. His column, "Philosophy in Action," appears in Guide for Spiritual Living: Science of Mind magazine. In 2015, he was inducted into the College of Bishops and Affirming Faith Leaders by the Fellowship of Affirming Ministries, and in 2016 was recognized with a Force for Good Award from Unity of Sacramento.

He has served as director of Strategic Alliances for the Centers for Spiritual Living, where he helped direct and coordinate partnerships between organizations to foster the creation of a world that works for all.

He and his wife, Patience, have two sons, William and Josh. Together they serve as his greatest cheerleaders and motivation for his work.

Learn more at www.revdavidalexander.com.

Made in the USA
Columbia, SC
24 March 2025